*Great Canadian Recipes*

# SUMMER
# BERRIES

## ELIZABETH BAIRD

James Lorimer & Company Ltd., Publishers
Toronto 2002

James Lorimer & Company Ltd. acknowledges the support of the Ontario Arts Council. We acknowledge the support of the Government of Canada through the Book Publishing Industry Development Program (BPIDP) for our publishing activities.

National Library of Canada Cataloguing in Publication


Baird, Elizabeth, 1939-
    Summer berries / Elizabeth Baird.


(Great Canadian recipes)
Includes index.
ISBN 1-55028-831-8


1. Cookery (Berries)  2. Cookery, Canadian.  I. Title. II. Series.

TX813.B4B35 2002              641.6'47              C2002-903082-X

Cover photo: Julian Beveridge

James Lorimer & Company Ltd., Publishers
35 Britain Street
Toronto, Ontario
M5A 1R7
www.lorimer.ca

Printed and bound in Canada.

# CONTENTS

# Acknowledgement

Once more I gratefully acknowledge the contribution of the Ontario Arts Council toward the preparation of the manuscript. The departments or ministries of agriculture in all the provinces and territories and in Ottawa were generous in responding to my requests about berries — their growing, harvesting, marketing and cooking.

I appreciate the research assistance of Shannon Ferrier and Rosemary Donegan, the testing help of Susan Carlton Thompson and Elizabeth Barry's skills as cook, critic and typist. George Baird has soldiered on through the feast and famine cycles that seem so much a part of the researching, testing and writing of any cookbook.

I deeply value the interest on the part of James Lorimer himself and his company in the awareness and development of Canadian cooking. I would especially like to thank Evelyn Ross, who has been involved in or responsible for the production of my three books.

E.B.

For Frank and Olive Davis

# INTRODUCTION

### SUMMER BERRIES

In a northern country like Canada, with a short but intense growing season, the splendour and variety of our summer fruit are all the more appreciated. I'm stretching the title *Summer Berries* on both counts — "summer" because the fruit featured ripens from May to October, and "berries" because there are recipes for rhubarb and red and black currants.

This book is a collection of the best traditional and regional recipes featuring Canadian native-grown soft fruits. This is not, however, a cookbook of wild berries, although they can be used in many of the recipes. The choice of recipes largely reflects the culinary and commercial predominance of the Big Five: strawberries, raspberries, blueberries, rhubarb and cranberries. Other berries such as bakeapples, partridgeberries, loganberries, blackberries, elderberries and saskatoons, although important regionally, are rarely available outside the areas where they grow; nevertheless I have included a few recipes for them and suggested ways that they can be substituted for other berries. Gooseberries and currants, on the other hand, enjoy an unjustifiably modest reputation throughout the country and I encourage you to try them.

### BAKEAPPLES

These are Canada's most exotic berry, found principally in the boggy areas of Newfoundland and Labrador. A bakeapple looks like a large, orange, softish raspberry and is known to Scandinavians as the cloudberry. It ripens from late July to mid-August.

Bakeapples are rather hard to find and time-consuming to pick, and are therefore available only rarely, and at high prices outside Newfoundland. The price gives the berry some commercial importance, encouraging the province to increase production. Bakeapples may be used in recipes calling for raspberries.

### BLACKBERRIES

Blackberries have been cultivated in North America since the 1800s; they are perhaps best known in British Columbia, where stands of the Himalayan blackberry, considered by some the finest of all varieties, have gone wild and grow not only in the country, as might be expected, but even in urban areas. Varieties of blackberries grow wild elsewhere in Canada and are available for home or commercial cultivation, but their commercial possibilities outside British Columbia are limited by their need for a relatively mild winter.

Blackberries look like large black raspberries but are in fact quite distinct from raspberries. Their cores stay inside the fruit when picked. They are exquisite fresh and make excellent wine, syrups, jams, puddings and baked goods of all sorts. They may be used in recipes calling for raspberries.

## BLUEBERRIES

Blueberries, the plump, sweet, steel-blue berries with a powder-like bloom, are among our all-time favourites. There are two sorts of blueberries: first, the sweet low-bush, indigenous to eastern and northern Canada. Its importance here is interesting when one considers that it is largely a wild berry, although a rather abundant one. Our largest acreage is on abandoned or exhausted farmland and stripped or burnt-over forest areas. Growers must periodically burn over the blueberry lands after harvesting to regenerate the bushes.

The second variety is the high-bush. It is grown extensively for processing in British Columbia and may become an interesting home garden crop as well as a profitable commercial one in milder parts of eastern Canada. I have found these berries rather flat-tasting but this is probably because they are picked before the characteristic blueberry flavour has had time to develop. They must ripen fully on the bush, for three to seven days after turning blue. Nevertheless, there is great potential for pick-your-own operations in high-bush blueberries, and a good outlook for the sale of fresh, frozen and processed berries of both varieties throughout Canada and abroad.

Although it varies according to region and variety, the blueberry season generally lasts from early or mid-July to the middle or end of September.

## CRANBERRIES

Cranberries are native to Canada and grow wild in many provinces, but the commercial cranberry crop is cultivated. There is cranberry production in Nova Scotia, Ontario, Quebec and the lower Fraser valley of British Columbia, areas where cool, moist conditions and acid soils prevail.

Cranberry growing is picturesque but expensive. The vines are planted in manmade paddies, surrounded by dikes and watered by a sophisticated irrigation system. In October, when the berries ripen, the paddies are flooded and the berries float up to the surface, where a mechanical plucker claws them off the vines. The harvested berries are then cleaned, dried and graded. The best berries are those with the most "bounce." Most Canadian cranberries are processed into sauces and other prepared foods; in some areas fresh cranberries from Canadian sources are simply unavailable.

## CURRANTS
Red and black currants have a long tradition of home cultivation throughout Canada. Even though we generally think of them as ingredients for jams and jellies, and maybe cordials or wines, they are also delightful ingredients in light summer sherbets, soups and cold puddings. July is the month for currants. Currants are becoming more available with the expansion of pick-your-own fruit farming.

## ELDERBERRIES
*Sambucus canadensis* is coming in from the wild. This berry is native to eastern Canada and has always been prolific in the wild; until recently there was little need for it to be cultivated. However, the use of herbicides has affected natural supplies, and commercial and garden growing methods are being developed.

The elderberry has a dual contribution to cooking. The flower makes a delightful fritter and adds beautiful perfume to gooseberry dishes, while the dark purple berry is a traditional ingredient in pies, jellies, jams, relishes and wine.

## GOOSEBERRIES
It's amazing that with all its prickles and time-consuming topping and tailing, this little berry is so well liked. Because of its tartness and acid it makes a first-rate jelly or jam and, sweetened with sugar and mellowed with cream, delightfully light summer desserts and pies as well. Gooseberries are usually only available in home gardens, independent fruit stores, roadside stands or pick-your-own operations. And here's good news: new varieties are being developed without thorns!

## LOGANBERRIES
This berry, a hybrid of the blackberry and raspberry, is available mainly

in British Columbia, from July to mid-August. It's a very large, deep red berry with small seeds and a sprightly acid flavour. It makes an excellent substitute for raspberries.

## PARTRIDGEBERRIES

Partridgeberries are in the cranberry family but are dark red, smaller and finer-flavoured. They are native to Newfoundland and Labrador, the Saguenay region of Quebec, Nova Scotia, where they are called foxberries, and the northern regions of the prairie provinces, where they are called mooseberries. They are the famous lingonberries of Scandinavian cuisine.

In Newfoundland they ripen in September, right after the blueberries, and are harvested and processed mainly for island consumption. Occasionally they are available elsewhere in Canada, in stores catering to Newfoundlanders, as jelly or frozen berries. There is considerable potential for developing this unique and profitable crop.

## RASPBERRIES

This is the berry with the most intensely divine flavour and perfume. Although raspberries grow wild and in cultivation over most of Canada, the greatest commercial production is around Clearbrook, in the Fraser valley. This area produces enough fresh berries to satisfy the B.C. market and thriving pick-your-own operations as well as processes 90 percent of Canada's commercial crop. Elsewhere raspberries have become such a luxury that they sell in tiny half-pint punnets at imported-delicacy prices. The problems that used to plague commercial raspberry growers — old plantings, virus disease, marketing problems, high production costs and the difficulty of getting harvest labour — seem at least partially solved. Improved disease-resistant stock, new herbicides, mechanical harvesting and the increasing popularity of the pick-your-own operations allow cautious optimism among raspberry growers and raspberry lovers alike.

Raspberries and strawberries are eminently well suited to the pick-your-own trend. The advantages to the grower are many: no more worries about finding good seasonal labour, nor about providing packing or the cold-storage facilities essential for raspberries. For the consumer, these berries are easy to pick and they can be sure of good quality at reasonable price by doing so.

Mid-July is the season for red raspberries and the related species of blackcaps and black, purple and yellow raspberries. New fall-bearing raspberries, which produce a crop in July and another in September, are of interest to home gardeners who can devote themselves to the extra care and extended harvesting they demand.

## RHUBARB

Rhubarb, native to central Asia, was introduced into Canada in the late eighteenth century. Going by the number of published recipes, rhubarb has got to be the favourite of all Canadian fruits. It is the first spring fruit and as true a harbinger of warm weather as a robin. It can be grown coast to coast, commercially and in home gardens. The rhubarb season begins in mid-February with specially forced pink rhubarb and continues into the spring and early summer with garden-harvested rhubarb. There is a promising commercial market for frozen rhubarb.

## SASKATOON BERRIES

*"On the Great Plains there is a shrub bearing a very sweet berry of a dark colour, much sought after; great quantities are dried by the Natives — and as much as possible is mixed to make Pemmecan."*

So wrote explorer David Thompson, describing the chewy "iron ration" that fuelled many a western explorer. Even now the saskatoon berry, more than any other fruit, brings back the taste of prairie summers. These berries do grow elsewhere in Canada, and are known as serviceberries or Juneberries, but nowhere are they so abundant or enjoyed as in the West. Saskatoons ripen in July and are usually eaten cooked, often combined with tarter fruit such as rhubarb or gooseberries, in pastry, drinks, puddings and of course, preserves. Saskatoons are a frequent substitute for blueberries.

## STRAWBERRIES

*"Doubtless God could have made a better berry than the Strawberry, but doubtless God never did."*

— Isaac Walton

Strawberries are the Canadian bargain berry and, indeed, our most important berry crop. Eastern Canada — with Ontario in the lead, Quebec next and then the Atlantic provinces — produces 70 percent of all Canadian strawberries. And strawberry production is on the rise due to improved varieties, disease-resistant plants, more efficient growing procedures and pest and weed control.

These technical conditions may seem a little mundane when we think of the pure pleasure this plump red berry affords us — fresh and in drinks, ice cream, sherbet, pies and preserves — but they are necessary to ensure consumers a reasonably priced berry and growers good return for their work. Canadian production is leaning away from processing and toward the fresh market, to such an extent that Ontario jam-makers have been forced to import berries to ensure a steady supply.

Strawberries are fairly easy to grow in home gardens. The gardener can choose from a variety of species to guarantee a supply of berries from mid-June to mid-July. There are even some everbearing berries that produce a June crop and a fall crop, or a single crop starting in June and ending with the frost.

# Care Of Summer Fruit

The very softest berries — raspberries, blackberries, strawberries and blueberries — spoil very quickly. Once home from the garden, the picking farm or the store, it is important that you sort the berries, spread them on shallow trays, cover lightly and chill. Of course it is best to use the berries immediately, but they will all keep for two to three days in the refrigerator. Blueberries keep a bit longer, four to five days. Wash the berries only just before using them, in a cold water bath. Hull strawberries at the last minute, too. Remove any spoiled or bruised berries and keep the berries dry at all times.

Berries like gooseberries, black currants, saskatoons, cranberries and partridgeberries are thicker-skinned; they only need to be covered lightly and kept chilled. They will keep up to a week. Red currants and elderberries should be treated the same way and can remain on their stems until they are needed. They should be used within three days and washed briefly before using.

Trim away the leaves and root ends of rhubarb stalks, wash them and wrap in a large plastic bag. Store in the refrigerator. Use the rhubarb within three to four days.

# Metric Measures

Because *Summer Berries* is being published in the transitional period between the imperial and metric systems, recipes are written with both sets of measurements and temperatures. Use the system most comfortable for you. The Canadian metric cooking system, like our old imperial system, is based on volume measurements. While most metric measures are similar to imperial, for the purposes of each recipe some measurements have had to be slightly adjusted.

# PIES AND PASTRIES

Pies and pastry-making are among the great strengths in Canadian cooking and the following recipes represent some of our finest — throughout the years and across the regions. In the first group in this chapter are the 2-crust flaky pastry kind, their tops glazed with cream and sugar granules and containing lots of berry filling; the summer picnic sort of pie, and just right to serve, freshly made, slathered with whipped cream or good vanilla ice cream. Then there are the recipes for the cool, uncooked glazed pies or the make-ahead chiffon sort. Berries are eminently well suited to these kinds of pie. Following them are custard pies and the scrumptious crumble pies. A pie to suit every occasion; pies to serve with pride.

## Assembling a Double-Crust Pie

There are a few tricks that will help keep the rich, runny juices of fruit pies sealed in.

The most important step is to make a superb seal around the edge of the pie. When you line the pie shell with the bottom crust, leave the pastry untrimmed and draped down over the edges of the pie plate. Fill the pie as directed in each recipe, then wet the pastry around the rim of the plate using a pastry brush or fingertips dipped in water. Lay the top layer of pastry over the filling and press the two layers together gently, just along the moistened rim. Using kitchen scissors or a sharp knife, trim the pastry evenly, leaving it still extending ½" (12 mm) over the rim of the plate. Now fold this lip of pastry up over the pastry on the rim and flute all the layers of pastry neatly together. This double fold is the most reliable way of preventing leaks.

All double-crust pies need steam vents. An old reliable vent is a circular hole, about the size of a quarter, cut in the very centre of the top pastry. And four or five ½" (12 mm) slashes radiating from the middle work very well indeed. Many cooks cut decorative patterns in the rolled-out pastry before it's placed over the filling. This is fine as long as the holes are close to the centre of the pie, and not down by the rim, where juices are more likely to escape.

# Glazing

All the 2-crust pies in this section can be baked without glazing. However, this extra step can make the classic double-crust pie into a spectacular-looking dessert.

The easiest glaze is 1 to 2 Tbs (15 to 25 mL) cream brushed over the entire surface of the pie and then 1 Tbs (15 mL) granulated sugar sprinkled over the pastry. The richer and heavier the cream and the coarser the sugar, the better the glaze. Always glaze just before baking.

The cream can be replaced by an egg white, whisked until foamy. Sprinkle on the sugar in the same way. One egg white will easily cover two pies. A third glaze, the richest, is made with an egg yolk beaten lightly with 1 tsp (5 mL) water and brushed over the pastry, followed by the sugar. The yellow yolk gives the pastry a head start in colouring. The yolk glaze will also cover two pies. The egg white and yolk glazes add a beautiful crunchy film to the top crust.

# Baking a Pie Shell Blind

Line the pie plate with pastry. Be sure not to stretch the pastry, but fit it neatly and comfortably into the plate, then trim around the edges with a sharp knife and flute. Now neatly line it with aluminum foil. Fill evenly with 4 cups (1 L) dried beans, split peas, lentils or rice. These beans or other things can be used over and over again for this purpose. Simply cool them after each use and store.

Bake the pie shell for 15 minutes at 425°F (220°C). Remove the foil and beans, cover the edges of the pastry with long strips of foil to prevent burning, and return it to the oven. Bake 3 to 5 minutes more to cook the base of the pie shell to an even golden colour. Cool.

# Flaky Pastry

5 cups (1.25 L) unsifted all-
purpose flour
2 tsp (10 mL) salt
½ tsp (3 mL) baking soda
1 Tbs (15 mL) granulated sugar

2 cups (500 mL) lard or shortening
1 egg, well beaten
1 Tbs (15 mL) vinegar
ice water

Stir together the flour, salt, baking soda and sugar in a very large bowl. Chop the lard into rough chunks and add to the flour. Working with a pastry blender or two knives, cut the lard into the dry ingredients until the mixture looks like corn kernels or rough rolled oats.

Pour the egg and vinegar into a liquid measure and fill to 1 cup (250 mL) with the ice water. Mix. Pour over the dry ingredients and use a fork to mix it in. Press into a ball.

Divide into 6 portions, form into balls, wrap in wax paper and chill. Freeze if desired. Follow baking instructions for each recipe.

Yields six 9" (1 L) or 10" (1.5 L) pie shells, or 3 shells and 3 tops.

# Sweet Pastry

1 cup (250 mL) unsifted all-
purpose flour
1 egg yolk
1 Tbs (15 mL) granulated sugar

½ cup (125 mL) soft butter
½ tsp (3 mL) grated lemon rind
1 to 2 Tbs (15 to 30 mL) ice water

Place the flour in a bowl. Make a well in the centre and put the egg yolk, sugar, butter and lemon rind into it. Using one hand, work these ingredients together in the centre, then gradually incorporate the flour. Add only as much water, if any, as is necessary to form a ball and absorb all the crumbs. Wrap and chill 1 hour. There is enough pastry for 1 large pie shell.

Because this pastry is made with sugar, it is somewhat more difficult to roll out than regular pastry. For best results, roll out the chilled pastry on a pastry cloth lightly dusted with flour and use a pastry sleeve over the rolling pin. Another guaranteed method is to roll it out between 2 long sheets of wax paper. To fit the rolled pastry into the pie plate, peel off the top layer of wax paper, then flip the paper, pastry side down, over the pie plate and peel off the remaining paper.

Fit the rolled pastry into a 9" or 10" (1 L or 1.5 L) pie plate. A shallow French tarte tin, flan pan or quiche pan is ideal. Bake according to instructions in each recipe.

Yields one 9" (1 L) or 10" (1.5 L) pie shell.

## Graham Cracker Crust

1½ cups (375 mL) graham
  cracker crumbs
¼ cup (50 mL) granulated sugar

½ tsp (2 mL) cinnamon (optional)
⅓ cup (75 mL) butter, melted

Combine the crumbs, sugar and cinnamon in a bowl. Thoroughly mix in the melted butter.

Press the crumbs firmly and evenly over the bottom and sides of a 9" or 10" (1 L or 1.5 L) pie plate. Bake at 350°F (180°C) 5 to 8 minutes for the thinner, larger pie shell, 8 to 10 minutes for the thicker, smaller shell. Cool completely before filling.

Just before serving the pie, wrap the bottom and sides of the pie plate with a hot, wet towel. Leave 2 to 3 minutes, remove the towel and serve. This little trick ensures clean, easily removed pie servings every time.

Yields one 9" or 10" (1 L or 1.5 L) pie shell.

## Almond Crumb Crust

¾ cup (175 mL) graham cracker
  crumbs
½ cup (125 mL) unblanched,
  very finely chopped almonds

3 Tbs (45 mL) granulated sugar
pinch of salt
⅓ cup (75 mL) butter, melted

Mix together in a bowl the cracker crumbs, almonds, sugar and salt. Mix the butter in with a fork. Spoon into a 9" or 10" (1 L or 1.5 L) pie plate; pat to form an even layer over the bottom and sides.

Bake at 350°F (180°C) for 4 to 6 minutes for the larger pie plate, 6 to 8 for the smaller. Cool before filling. The bigger pie crust is thinner and bakes more quickly.

Yields one 9" or 10" (1 L or 1.5 L) pie shell.

# Classic Raspberry Pie With Mint

Because of the rapid increase in the price of raspberries, this old-time classic has become a true luxury dessert. This pie alone, however, makes cultivating raspberries or planning a day at a pick-your-own raspberry farm worthwhile.

sufficient pastry for a 2-crust 10" (1.5 L) pie

FILLING:
4 cups (1 L) raspberries
¾ cup (175 mL) granulated sugar
2 Tbs (30 mL) cornstarch
1 tsp (5 mL) lemon juice
¼ tsp (2 mL) finely chopped
   fresh mint (optional)
1 Tbs (15 mL) butter

GLAZE:
1 Tbs (15 mL) light cream
1 Tbs (15 mL) granulated sugar

Line the pie plate with pastry but do not trim. Preheat oven to 425°F (220°C).
   To make the filling, place the raspberries in a large bowl. Combine the sugar and the cornstarch, pour over the berries and toss very gently. Put into the pie shell. Sprinkle on the lemon juice and mint; dot with the butter.
   Cover and glaze according to instructions on page 12.
   Bake 15 minutes; then reduce heat to 350°F (180°C) and bake 35 minutes more, or until the fruit is tender and the crust golden. Serve with good vanilla ice cream.

Yields 6 to 8 servings, depending on the desire for raspberries.

# Blackberry Pie

Proceed as for the Classic Raspberry Pie with Mint, substituting blackberries for the raspberries. Omit the mint.

# Raspberry and Blueberry Cipâte

This Québecois pie was originally baked in a cast-iron pot. The filling is just runny enough to be convincing and has a fresh but somewhat mysterious taste of raspberries plus.

sufficient pastry for a 2-crust 9" (1 L) pie

FILLING:
1½ cups (375 mL) raspberries
2 cups (500 mL) blueberries
⅔ cup (150 mL) granulated sugar
3 Tbs (45 mL) all-purpose flour
½ tsp (3 mL) grated lemon rind
2 Tbs (25 mL) lemon juice
2 Tbs (25 mL) butter

GLAZE:
1 Tbs (15 mL) light cream
1 Tbs (15 mL) granulated sugar

Line the pie shell with pastry but do not trim off the excess. Preheat oven to 425°F (220°C).

To make the filling, toss together lightly the berries, sugar, flour and lemon rind. Pour into the pie shell. Mound up slightly in the middle. Sprinkle on the lemon juice and dot with butter.

Finish assembling and glazing the pie according to the instructions on page 12. Bake for 15 minutes, then reduce heat to 350°F (180°C) and bake 30 minutes more. The pie should be beautifully bronzed and the filling bubbling. Serve while still just warm with scoops of good vanilla ice cream.

Yields 6 generous pieces.

# Classic Wild Blueberry Pie

At Grandview Lodge near Orillia, Ontario, one of the activities for the guests' children used to be blueberry picking. We kids would all pile into the back of a pickup truck and off we would go to compete with the black flies, heat and bears for a pail of berries. Of course, the treat at the end of this was the pie — or, if we were lucky, pies — baked by the lodge pastry chef.

sufficient pastry for a deep 2-crust 9" (1 L) pie

FILLING:
4 cups (1 L) blueberries
½ cup (125 mL) granulated sugar
2 Tbs (30 mL) cornstarch
2 tsp (10 mL) lemon juice
2 Tbs (25 mL) butter

GLAZE:
1 Tbs (15 mL) light cream
1 Tbs (15 mL) granulated sugar

Line the pie plate with pastry but do not trim the edges. Preheat oven to 425°F (220°C).

To make the filling place the blueberries, sugar and cornstarch in a large bowl. Toss together thoroughly and pour into the pie shell. Mound up slightly in the middle. Sprinkle on the lemon juice and dot with the butter.

Cover and glaze according to instructions on page 12.

Bake for 15 minutes, then reduce heat to 375°F (190°C) and bake 30 to 35 minutes more, or until the crust is a lovely golden brown and the filling is beginning to bubble up through the slashed holes. Serve with good vanilla ice cream.

Yields 6 to 8 servings.

# Gingery Elderberry and Peach Pie

The sour cream and peaches provide a luscious foil to the crunchy elderberries and the bits of piquant ginger.

sufficient pastry for a 2-crust 9" (1 L) pie

FILLING:
2 cups (500 mL) sliced peaches
2 cups (500 mL) elderberries
⅔ cup (150 mL) granulated sugar
3 Tbs (45 mL) all-purpose flour
4 tsp (20 mL) very finely chopped
   crystallized or drained
   preserved ginger
2 Tbs (25 mL) butter
3 Tbs (45 mL) sour cream

GLAZE:
1 Tbs (15 mL) light cream
1 Tbs (15 mL) granulated sugar

Line the pie plate with pastry but do not trim off the edges. Preheat oven to 425ºF (220ºC).

To make the filling, arrange the peaches in the bottom of the shell. Toss together the elderberries, sugar and flour; spoon over the peaches. Sprinkle on the ginger, and dot the butter and sour cream evenly over the fruit.

Cover and glaze according to the instructions on page 12. Bake for 15 minutes, then reduce heat to 350ºF (180ºC) for 30 to 35 minutes more. The crust should be golden and the filling bubbling and tender. Delicious alone or with lightly whipped cream.

Yields 6 good servings.

# Classic Gooseberry Pie

This is a pie I would encourage cooks to try. It's an extremely fine one, just tart enough but with a delicate taste. Use green or ripe pink berries, or a combination of both stages of gooseberries, for the filling.

sufficient pastry for a 2-crust 9" (1 L) pie

FILLING:
1 cup (250 mL) granulated sugar
2 Tbs (30 mL) all-purpose flour
4 cups (1 L) gooseberries,
  topped and tailed
½ tsp (3 mL) grated orange rind

2 Tbs (30 mL) butter, melted

GLAZE:
egg white or 1 Tbs (15 mL) light
  cream
1 Tbs (15 mL) granulated sugar

Line the pie plate with pastry but do not trim the edges. Preheat oven to 425°F (220°C).

To make the filling, combine the sugar and flour and spread half over the bottom of the pie shell. Spoon in the gooseberries evenly, followed by the rest of the sugar and flour. Sprinkle on the orange rind and butter.

Cover and glaze according to instructions on page 12.

Bake for 15 minutes, then reduce heat to 375°F (190°C) and bake 35 minutes more, or until the crust is golden and the filling begins to bubble up.

Yields 6 to 8 servings.


# Cranberry Mincemeat Pie

sufficient pastry for a 2-crust 9" (1 L) pie

FILLING:
1 cup (250 mL) peeled and
  cored finely chopped apples
  or pears
3 cups (750 mL) Cranberry
  Mincemeat (page 94)
½ cup (125 mL) blanched
  chopped almonds

2 Tbs (25 mL) sherry
2 Tbs (25 mL) butter

GLAZE:
1 Tbs (15 mL) light cream
1 Tbs (15 mL) granulated sugar

Line a pie plate with pastry. Do not trim the edges. Preheat oven to 425°F (220°C).

To make the filling, mix the apples, mincemeat, almonds and sherry. Spoon into the pie shell, heaping it up slightly in the middle. Dot with the butter.

Cover, flute and glaze according to instructions on page 12.

Bake for 10 minutes, then reduce heat to 350°F (180°C) and bake for 30 minutes longer. The crust should be golden brown, and the mincemeat bubbling up through the slashes. The pie is best when served while still fairly hot, with scoops of vanilla ice cream.

Yields 6 to 8 rich portions.

# Partridgeberry Tart

This is a shallow, fragrant lattice pie that can be made with any tart berry jam: raspberry, blackberry, cranberry or, in Newfoundland, bakeapple. A layer of blanched slivered almonds sprinkled over the bottom crust couldn't hurt. Whipped cream is a must with this rich pie.

sufficient pastry for a shallow 2-crust 10" (1.5 L) pie

1 egg yolk
1⅓ cups (325 mL) partridge-
    berry jam
1 tsp (5 mL) granulated sugar

Line the pie plate with pastry but do not trim. Preheat oven to 400°F (200°C).

Beat the egg yolk lightly. Brush some of it over the pastry on the bottom, sides and rim of the shell. Spoon the jam into the shell, smoothing it evenly with the back of the spoon.

Roll out sufficient pastry for the top. Cut into even strips about ½" (12 mm) wide, using a crimp-edged pastry wheel if possible. Lay them all in one direction over the jam, leaving only about ⅛" (3 mm) between strips. Trim the ends and the overhang from the bottom crust. Press together firmly with a fork. Brush the pastry with the remaining egg yolk and sprinkle the sugar evenly over the top.

Bake for 20 to 25 minutes, or until the pastry is a perfect medium brown. Serve with a bowl of unsweetened whipped cream.

Yields about 8 servings.

# Saskatoon Pie

Try to use tarter red saskatoons for this pie. For them, ⅔ cup (150 mL) sugar is necessary; for the darker, riper berries, reduce the quantity of sugar to ½ cup (125 mL).

sufficient pastry for a 2-crust 9" (1 L) pie

FILLING:
4 cups (1 L) saskatoons
2 Tbs (25 mL) apple juice
1 tsp (5 mL) grated lemon rind
2 Tbs (25 mL) lemon juice
½ to ⅔ cup (125 to 150 mL)
   firmly packed brown sugar
4 tsp (20 mL) all-purpose flour
2 Tbs (25 mL) butter

GLAZE:
1 Tbs (15 mL) light cream
1 Tbs (15 mL) granulated sugar

Line the pie plate with pastry but do not trim. Preheat oven to 425°F (220°C).

To make the filling, place the saskatoons, apple juice, lemon rind and juice in a medium saucepan. Cover and bring to the boil over high heat, then reduce heat and simmer 3 to 5 minutes, or until just barely tender. Remove from the heat. Mix the brown sugar and flour together; stir into the berry mixture with the butter. Cool.

Pour the filling into the pie shell. Finish assembling and glazing according to instructions on page 12.

Bake for 15 minutes, then reduce the heat to 350°F (180°C) and bake 30 minutes, or until the crust is thoroughly golden.

Cool and serve with good vanilla ice cream.

Yields 6 generous servings.

# Saskatoon Rhubarb Pie

Proceed as for Saskatoon Pie, replacing 1 cup (250 mL) of the saskatoons with finely chopped rhubarb. Use the larger quantity of sugar.

# Almond Red Currant Pie

Some people find red currant seeds too crunchy, but the addition of the slivered almonds gives this pie extra texture and the net result is most pleasing.

sufficient pastry for a 2-crust 10" (1.5 L) pie

FILLING:
¾ cup (175 mL) blanched
  slivered almonds
4 cups (1 L) stemmed red currants
½ tsp (3 mL) almond extract
¼ cup (60 mL) all-purpose flour
1¾ cups (425 mL) granulated
  sugar
2 Tbs (30 mL) butter

GLAZE:
1 egg white or 1 Tbs (15 mL) light
  cream
1 Tbs (15 mL) granulated sugar

Line the pie plate with pastry. Do not trim. Preheat oven to 425ºF (220ºC).

For the filling, scatter the almonds onto the pastry. Combine the next 4 ingredients in a bowl, then spread over the almonds. Dot with the butter.

Cover and glaze according to the instructions on page 12. Bake 15 minutes, then reduce heat to 350ºF (180ºC) and bake 35 to 40 minutes more, or until the pastry is golden and the filling bubbling.

Yields 8 generous servings, 10 with good vanilla ice cream.

# Glazed Blueberry Pie

I have suggested two quantities of whole uncooked blueberries, 2 cups (500 mL) for the 9" (1 L) and 3 cups (750 mL) for the 10" (1.5 L) pie. This is the pie for the cook who wants to retain the fresh flavour of the berries.

sufficient pastry for a 1-crust 9" or 10" (1 L or 1.5 L) pie or 1 recipe of
    Sweet Pastry (page 14)

¾ cup (175 mL) granulated sugar
3 Tbs (45 mL) cornstarch
⅛ tsp (0.5 mL) salt
⅓ cup (75 mL) cold water
½ tsp (3 mL) grated lemon rind

4 to 5 cups (1 to 1.25 L) blueberries
1 Tbs (15 mL) butter
2 Tbs (30 mL) lemon juice
1 cup (250 mL) heavy cream

Bake the pie shell blind, according to the instructions on page 13.

Combine the sugar, cornstarch and salt in a heavy-bottomed saucepan. Stir in the water, lemon rind and 2 cups (500 mL) of the blueberries. Place over medium-low heat and simmer gently about 10 minutes, or until the mixture has thickened and cleared. Remove from the heat, mix in the butter and lemon juice and cool slightly.

Spread the remaining blueberries evenly over the bottom of the baked pie shell. Spoon the cooked berry glaze over the berries. Cool.

To serve, whip the cream and spoon or pipe attractively over the top.

Yields 8 servings.

# Glazed Strawberry Pie

This was *the* Canadian strawberry pie in the 1950s. It's a recipe that turns up time and time again when I ask people for their favourite strawberry pie.

sufficient pastry for 1-crust 10" (1.5 L) pie, or 1 recipe of Sweet Pastry (page 14), or 1 recipe of Graham Cracker Crust (page 15) or Almond Crumb Crust (page 15)

5 cups (1.25 L) hulled strawberries
¾ cup (175 mL) water
3 Tbs (45 mL) cornstarch
1 cup (250 mL) granulated sugar
1 tsp (5 mL) lemon juice

1 Tbs (15 mL) brandy or almond liqueur, or 2 drops almond extract
1 cup (250 mL) heavy cream

Bake the pastry shell blind, according to the instructions on page 13; or bake the Graham Cracker Crust or Almond Crumb Crust according to their recipes.

Pick out 3 cups (750 mL) of the finest strawberries and place on a rack or towelling to dry. Crush the remaining berries in a heavy-bottomed saucepan, and add the water. Combine the cornstarch and sugar; mix into the berries and water. Cook over medium-low heat until thickened and clear, about 10 minutes. Cool slightly, then add the lemon juice and brandy.

Arrange the berries, tips up, in the pie shell. Spoon the glaze evenly over the berries. Cool. The pie can be made up to this point, and a delay of up to 2 hours will not spoil it. At serving time, whip the cream and pipe or spoon around the rim of the pie.

Yields 6 to 8 servings.

# Strawberry Bavarian Pie

1 recipe of Graham Cracker Crust (page 15), or 1 recipe of Almond Crumb Crust (page 15)

3 cups (750 mL) hulled strawberries
¾ cup (175 mL) granulated sugar
2 Tbs (25 mL) all-purpose flour
1 Tbs (15 mL) unflavoured gelatin

½ cup (125 mL) cold water
2 eggs, separated
pinch of salt
pinch of cream of tartar
1 cup (250 mL) heavy cream

Prepare and bake crust in 9" (1 L) pan.

Set aside 1½ cups (375 mL) of the finest berries, of more or less even size. Mash or purée the remainder using a coarse sieve, the medium disk of a food mill, a blender or a food processor. Place in a medium bowl and mix in ¼ cup (50 mL) of the sugar. Leave at room temperature and stir periodically to dissolve the sugar.

Blend ¼ cup (50 mL) of the sugar with the flour and gelatin in a saucepan; mix in the water. Add the egg yolks and whisk together thoroughly. Place over low heat and cook, whisking constantly, until the mixture thickens. Remove from the heat, cool 10 minutes and beat into the berry purée. Chill until partially set, about 30 to 40 minutes.

In a large bowl beat the egg whites, salt and cream of tartar at low speed until frothy. Increase the speed to high and beat to soft peaks. Begin adding the remaining sugar, still beating until the meringue stands in firm glossy peaks.

Whip ½ cup (125 mL) of the cream. Add a quarter of the meringue to the strawberry mixture and stir in, then fold in the whipped cream. Scrape this all onto the remaining egg whites and fold in thoroughly. Spoon into the pie shell, even the top and chill until firm, about 2 hours.

Arrange the reserved berries whole, tip up, around the edge of the pie and in the centre. Whip the remaining cream and pipe rosettes beside the berries.

Yields 6 servings.

# Strawberry Cream Pie

The "cream" means a pastry cream or custard and shows the French influence in this 1940s recipe. It's equally good with raspberries, blackberries or blueberries for the top layer. Because the custard filling will make the crust soggy, plan to eat this pie within an hour of making it. If that just won't work, however, have everything except the glaze prepared and assemble and glaze at the last minute. It's worth making everybody wait for this dessert.

1 recipe of Sweet Pastry (page 14)

FILLING:
1¼ cups (300 mL) milk
1 Tbs (15 mL) cornstarch
⅓ cup (75 mL) granulated sugar
⅛ tsp (0.5 mL) salt
2 Tbs (30 mL) milk
2 egg yolks, well beaten
½ tsp (3 mL) vanilla

2½ cups (625 mL) hulled
  strawberries

GLAZE:
½ cup (125 mL) Red Currant
  Jelly (page 105)
1 Tbs (15 mL) brandy or orange
  juice

Prepare Sweet Pastry and line a 9" (1 L) pie plate; bake blind (see page 13).

   To make the filling, scald the 1¼ cups (300 mL) of milk in the top of a double boiler over direct medium heat. Combine the cornstarch, sugar and salt, and blend in the 2 Tbs (30 mL) milk; stir into the scalded milk. Cook over boiling water until thickened and the taste of cornstarch is lost, about 8 minutes. Pour about a quarter of this custard into the egg yolks, beating constantly, then pour it all back into the hot mixture, continuing to beat. Cook over simmering water until thickened, about 4 minutes, stirring frequently. Remove from the heat, stir in the vanilla and chill.

   Spread the custard over the bottom of the pie shell. Place the berries, tips up, in the custard. Melt the jelly with the brandy over medium heat and brush or spoon gently over berries. Best served within an hour.

Yields 6 generous servings.

# Cranberry Chiffon Pie

1 recipe of Graham Cracker Crust (page 15), or 1 recipe of Almond
   Crumb Crust (page 15)

FILLING:
2½ cups (625 mL) cranberries
¾ cup (175 mL) Cranberry Juice
   (page 111), or water
3 eggs
1 cup (250 mL) granulated sugar
1 Tbs (15 mL) unflavoured
   gelatin
2 Tbs (30 mL) water

1 Tbs (15 mL) lemon juice
1 tsp (5 mL) grated orange rind
1 tsp (5 mL) orange liqueur
   (optional)
pinch of salt
pinch of cream of tartar

GARNISH:
½ cup (125 mL) heavy cream

Prepare and bake the crust in a 9" (1 L) pan.

To make the filling, combine the berries and juice in a heavy-bottomed saucepan and bring to the boil over high heat. Immediately reduce the heat; simmer gently 8 to 10 minutes, or until the berries are tender. Remove from the heat and remove 15 of the berries with a slotted spoon. Set them on a plate and cool; cover gently with plastic wrap.

Press the remaining berries and juice through a sieve or the fine disk of a food mill. Discard the seeds and skins. Wash out the saucepan and return the cranberry purée to it.

Separate the eggs. Drop the whites into a large bowl and reserve, and the yolks into a medium bowl. Whisk the yolks with ½ cup (125 mL) of the sugar, then stir into the cranberry purée. Place over simmering water or low heat and cook 4 to 6 minutes, or until thickened, stirring frequently.

While the berry-yolk mixture cooks, sprinkle the gelatin into the water, stir and let soften. Remove the berry purée from the heat, blend in the softened gelatin and mix until all the granules have dissolved. Add the lemon juice, orange rind and liqueur. Scrape into a medium bowl and chill until thickened and partially set, about 45 minutes to an hour.

Sprinkle the salt and cream of tartar over the egg whites. Beat at low speed until frothy, then increase the speed to high and beat to the soft-peak stage. Start adding the last ½ cup (125 mL) of the sugar, continuing to beat until the meringue is firm and glossy. Stir about a quarter of this meringue into the cranberry mixture, then scrape this cranberry custard onto the rest of the meringue and fold in gently but thoroughly.

Pile into the pie shell. Smooth the top and chill 4 hours, or until quite firm. To serve, whip the cream and pipe 12 rosettes evenly round the edge of the pie and a big rosette in the middle. Centre one of the reserved cranberries in each small side rosette and 3 in the middle rosette. Yields 6 generous servings.

# Raspberry Cream Chiffon Pie

A very pretty pie. For an added touch, toast ¼ cup (50 mL) sliced almonds, cool and sprinkle onto the rosettes of whipped cream.

1 recipe of Graham Cracker Crust (page 15), or 1 recipe of Almond Crumb Crust (page 15)

3 cups (750 mL) raspberries
¾ cup (175 mL) granulated sugar
¾ cup (175 mL) water
1 Tbs (15 mL) unflavoured gelatin
½ tsp (2 mL) grated lemon rind

1 Tbs (15 mL) lemon juice
2 egg whites
pinch of salt
pinch of cream of tartar
1 cup (250 mL) heavy cream

Prepare and bake crust in a 9" (1 L) pan.

Reserve 1 cup (250 mL) of the best even-sized berries. Crush or purée the rest using a fork, blender or food processor. Place in a medium bowl, mix in ½ cup (125 mL) of the sugar and set aside at room temperature. Stir periodically.

Measure the water into a small saucepan, sprinkle on the gelatin, stir well and place over low heat. Heat and stir until all the gelatin granules have dissolved. Add, with the lemon rind and juice, to the puréed raspberries, and mix well. Chill until partially set, about 45 to 60 minutes.

Place the egg whites in a large bowl; add the salt and cream of tartar and beat at low speed until frothy. Increase speed to high and beat to soft peaks. Add the remaining ¼ cup (50 mL) sugar, continuing to beat. Stop when the meringue stands in firm, glossy peaks.

Whip half the cream. Stir about a quarter of the meringue into the raspberry mixture, fold in the whipped cream and then fold this all into the remaining egg whites.

Spoon into the pie shell and chill until firm, about 2 hours. To serve, arrange the remaining berries around the edge and centre of the pie. Whip the remaining cream and pipe rosettes beside the berries.

Yields 6 generous servings.

# Blueberry Custard Pie

sufficient pastry for a deep 1-crust 9" (1 L) pie

FILLING:
2 cups (500 mL) blueberries
½ cup (125 mL) granulated sugar
2 Tbs (30 mL) all-purpose flour
¼ tsp (1 mL) salt
½ tsp (3 mL) grated lemon rind
1 Tbs (15 mL) lemon juice

CUSTARD:
2 egg yolks
¼ cup (50 mL) granulated sugar
1 cup (250 mL) light cream
freshly grated nutmeg

Line a pie shell with the pastry. Preheat oven to 425°F (220°C).

To make the filling, measure the blueberries into a medium bowl. Combine the sugar, flour, salt and lemon rind, toss with the berries and pour into the pie shell. Sprinkle on the lemon juice. Arrange the berries evenly.

Line the edges of the pastry with strips of aluminum foil to keep them from browning too fast. Bake for 15 minutes, then reduce heat to 350°F (180°C) and bake for another 15 minutes.

While the pie is baking, prepare the custard by beating the yolks and sugar together, then mixing in the cream. Spoon the custard gently over the berries in the baked pie. Grate a light film of nutmeg over the top.

Continue baking at 350°F (180°C) for 20 to 25 minutes. The custard is ready when the tip of a knife inserted into it comes out clean. Cool and serve freshly made.

Yields 6 servings.

# Red Currant Custard Pie

This kind of pie, with a layer of fruit covered with a rich baked custard, is a classic in Canadian cooking. This particular recipe is from a 1930s Alberta collective cookbook. Ripe gooseberries, topped and tailed, are just as tasty as red currants in this pie. Plan to eat it as soon as it's cool from the oven.

sufficient pastry for a 1-crust 10" (1.5 L) pie

FILLING:
3 cups (750 mL) stemmed red
   currants
2 Tbs (30 mL) all-purpose flour
¾ cup (175 mL) granulated sugar
½ tsp (3 mL) grated orange rind

CUSTARD:
2 eggs, well beaten
¾ cup (175 mL) light cream or
   milk
⅓ cup (75 mL) granulated sugar
¼ tsp (1 mL) cardamom

Line a pie plate with the pastry. Preheat oven to 425°F (220°C).

To prepare the filling, combine the currants, flour, sugar and orange rind in a medium bowl. Spoon into the pie shell. Bake for 15 minutes, then reduce heat to 350°F (180°C) and bake 15 minutes more.

Meanwhile prepare the custard. Combine the eggs, cream and sugar. Remove the pie from the oven and spoon the custard mixture gently over the currants. Sprinkle the cardamom over the surface. Return to the oven and bake 20 to 25 minutes more, or until the tip of a knife inserted in the custard comes out clean. The crust should be a golden brown and the currants bubbling up here and there through the custard.

Yields 8 servings.

# Old-Fashioned Rhubarb Custard Pie

There are eggs but no milk in this pie; the juiciness of the rhubarb more than compensates. This is a good pie to serve to skeptics who think there's no such thing as Canadian cooking.

sufficient pastry for a deep 1-crust 10" (1.5 L) pie

¼ cup (50 mL) unsifted all-purpose flour
1¼ cups (300 mL) granulated sugar
5 cups (1.25 L) chopped rhubarb, in ½" (12 mm) pieces

2 eggs
½ tsp (3 mL) grated lemon rind
2 Tbs (25 mL) lemon juice
2 Tbs (30 mL) melted butter

Line a pie plate with the pastry. Preheat oven to 450°F (230°C).

Combine the flour and sugar. Sprinkle a quarter of the mixture over the bottom of the pie shell. Cover with chopped rhubarb. Mix the remaining flour and sugar with the eggs, rind, juice and melted butter. Beat enough to mix together and spread evenly over the rhubarb.

Bake 10 minutes, then reduce the heat to 350°F (180°C) and continue baking 25 to 30 minutes, or until the crust is golden, the rhubarb soft and the custardy filling set. If the crust, especially along the rim, browns too quickly, cover loosely with strips of aluminum foil. Remove when the pie is baked. This one's best when freshly made.

Yields 6 to 8 servings.

# Rhubarb Cream Streusel Pie

From Sebringville, Ontario, an early spring version of the Mennonite schnitz apple pie.

sufficient pastry for a 1-crust 10" (1.5 L) pie

FILLING:
1¼ cups (300 mL) granulated sugar
¼ cup (50 mL) unsifted all-purpose flour
¾ cup (175 mL) sour cream
1 egg yolk
4 cups (1 L) diced rhubarb, in ½" (12 mm) pieces

STREUSEL TOPPING:
½ cup (125 mL) unsifted all-purpose flour
½ cup (125 mL) firmly packed brown sugar
½ tsp (3 mL) cinnamon or freshly grated nutmeg
¼ cup (50 mL) cold butter

Line a pie plate with the pastry. Preheat oven to 425ºF (220ºC).

To make the filling, place the sugar, flour, sour cream, egg yolk and rhubarb in a large bowl. Mix thoroughly, then spoon into the pie shell.

To make the topping, mix the dry ingredients in a medium bowl. Using a pastry blender or two knives, cut the butter into the mixture until it is crumbly. Spoon evenly over the rhubarb.

Bake for 15 minutes, then reduce heat to 350ºF (180ºC) and bake 30 minutes more, or until the crumble top is golden and crisp, and the rhubarb is tender. Serve warm or cold.

Yields 8 servings.

# Blueberry Nut Streusel Pie

To make this pie with saskatoons, add ¼ cup (50 mL) orange juice or water to the filling.

sufficient pastry for a deep 1-crust 9" (1 L) pie

FILLING:
4 cups (1 L) blueberries
⅔ cup (150 mL) granulated sugar
¼ cup (50 mL) unsifted all-purpose flour
1 tsp (5 mL) grated lemon rind
1 Tbs (15 mL) lemon juice

STREUSEL TOPPING:
½ cup (125 mL) unsifted all-purpose flour
½ tsp (2 mL) cinnamon
6 Tbs (100 mL) firmly packed brown sugar
¼ cup (50 mL) cold butter
¼ cup (50 mL) chopped almonds or pecans (optional)

Line a pie plate with the pastry. Preheat oven to 425°F (220°C).

To make the filling, place the berries in a large bowl. Combine the sugar and flour, tip onto the berries and toss to distribute evenly. Pour into the pie shell. Sprinkle the lemon rind and juice over the top. Arrange the filling evenly.

For the topping, combine the flour, cinnamon and brown sugar. Cut in the butter to make pea-sized crumbs. Add the nuts. Spoon the topping over the berries, pressing down slightly to even out the top.

Bake for 15 minutes, then reduce the heat to 350°F (180°C) and bake 35 to 40 minutes more. The crumb streusel should be bronzed and the filling bubbling up. Serve warm or cold.

Yields 6 generous servings.

# CAKES, COOKIES, MUFFINS, BREADS AND PANCAKES

## Blueberry Orange Cake

Blueberry cakes are special favourites in Atlantic Canada. Recipe books there can be counted on to include at least one version of this classic. This recipe shows off the berries baked in a layer running through the centre of an orange bundt cake. Westerners can substitute saskatoons.

BATTER:
½ cup (125 mL) butter
1 cup (250 mL) granulated sugar
1 egg
2 tsp (10 mL) grated orange rind
2 cups (500 mL) sifted all-
  purpose flour
1 Tbs (15 mL) baking powder
½ tsp (2 mL) salt
1 cup (250 mL) blueberries or
  saskatoons

½ cup (125 mL) orange juice
½ cup (125 mL) milk

ICING:
3 Tbs (45 mL) brown sugar
1 tsp (5 mL) grated orange rind
3 Tbs (45 mL) orange juice
1 Tbs (15 mL) orange liqueur,
  gin, or extra orange juice

Butter a 9" (2 L) tube or bundt pan. Dust with flour and tip out the excess. Preheat oven to 350°F (180°C).

To make the batter, cream the butter, add the sugar and beat until light and fluffy. Add the egg and grated rind. Beat well.

Sift together the flour, baking powder and salt. Spoon out 1 Tbs (15 mL) and dredge the fruit with it. Stir a third of the sifted dry ingredients into the creamed mixture, then the orange juice, followed by a second portion of flour, then the milk and the last third.

Spoon half the batter into the tube pan. Distribute the berries over the batter, keeping them centred ½" (12 mm) from the edges of the pan. Spoon the rest of the batter over the berries. Tap the pan once lightly on the counter.

Bake for 45 minutes, or until a skewer inserted in the middle of the cake comes out clean. Cool 10 minutes in the pan, then turn out onto a flat serving plate.

Combine the ingredients for the icing and drizzle over the cake while it is still slightly warm. Yields 12 servings.

# Blueberry Buckle

Even though the word "buckle" identifies this cake as a Down East specialty, blueberries are Canada-wide and Westerners can substitute saskatoons.

CAKE:
½ cup (125 mL) butter
½ cup (125 mL) firmly packed
  brown sugar
1 egg
1 tsp (5 mL) vanilla
2 cups (500 mL) sifted all-
  purpose flour
1 Tbs (15 mL) baking powder
½ tsp (3 mL) salt

¾ cup (175 mL) milk
3 cups (750 mL) blueberries

TOPPING:
½ cup (125 mL) firmly packed
  brown sugar
6 Tbs (100 mL) all-purpose flour
½ tsp (3 mL) cinnamon
¼ cup (60 mL) cold butter

Butter an 8" x 12" (3 L) cake tin. Preheat oven to 350°F (180°C).

To make the cake batter, cream the butter, then beat in the brown sugar, egg and vanilla. Sift together the flour, baking powder and salt. Mix into the batter in 3 portions, alternately with the milk, in 2 portions. Spread evenly in the cake pan.

Pour the blueberries over the batter in an even layer. Press down very lightly.

To make the topping, combine the brown sugar, flour and cinnamon. Cut in the cold butter, working until the mixture is crumbly. Sprinkle evenly over the berries.

Bake 50 to 55 minutes, or until the crumble top is light golden and the berries tender, and a skewer inserted into the cake comes out clean. Leave the buckle in the pan.

Serve while still warm, with whipped cream, sour cream or good vanilla ice cream. Yields 10 to 12 servings.

# Cranberry Coffee Cake

Proceed exactly as for Blueberry Buckle but substitute cranberries and increase the sugar in the topping to ¾ cup (175 mL).

Use other tart fruit such as partridgeberries, red currants or finely chopped rhubarb instead of the cranberries for a variety of terrific toppings.

# Imperial Blackberry Cheesecake

Based on a recipe that was one of the 1968 CNE Baking Day winners, this is the deluxe version of cheesecake. Substitute raspberries or strawberries in season, or use the topping from Cranberry Glazed Cheesecake, page 38, or serve unglazed and pass any one of the fruit sauces, pages 74-77.

CRUST:
½ cup (125 mL) crushed graham
  cracker crumbs plus ½ cup
  (125 mL) finely chopped nuts
1 Tbs (15 mL) granulated sugar
1 Tbs (15 mL) grated orange rind
3 Tbs (45 mL) melted butter

FILLING:
4 eggs
pinch of salt
pinch of cream of tartar
1 cup (250 mL) granulated sugar
1 tsp (5 mL) vanilla
1½ lb (750 g) cream cheese,
  at room temperature

SOUR CREAM TOPPING:
2 cups (500 mL) sour cream
¼ cup (50 mL) granulated sugar
1 tsp (5 mL) vanilla

BERRY GLAZE:
4½ cups (1.125 L) blackberries,
  raspberries, hulled strawberries or other berries
2 tsp (10 mL) unflavoured gelatin
¼ cup (50 mL) water
2 Tbs (25 mL) orange juice

Lightly butter the bottom and sides of a 10″ (3.5 L) spring-form pan. Preheat oven to 325°F (160°C).

To prepare the crust, combine thoroughly the crumbs, sugar, orange rind and melted butter. Pour into the pan and press into an even layer over the bottom of the pan only. Set aside.

To make the filling, separate the eggs, dropping the whites into a large bowl and the yolks into a medium bowl. Sprinkle the salt and cream of tartar over the whites. Beat at low speed until foamy, then increase speed to high and beat to soft peaks. Continue beating, gradually adding ¼ cup (50 mL) of the sugar to form a firm meringue.

Beat the egg yolks with the remaining sugar and add the vanilla. Mash the cream cheese and beat until smooth; blend in the yolk mixture. Stir about a quarter of the meringue into the cheese, then turn all the cheese mixture into the meringue and fold together gently but thoroughly. Pour over the crust in the pan. Bake for 45 to 50 minutes, or until a skewer inserted into the middle comes out clean. Remove from the oven and increase the heat to 375ºF (190ºC).

To make the sour cream topping, combine the sour cream, sugar and vanilla. Spoon evenly over the cheesecake and bake for 8 minutes. Cool thoroughly in the pan.

To make the berry glaze, press 1½ cups (375 mL) of the berries through a sieve to extract the juice. There should be ⅔ cup (150 mL). With blueberries, it may be necessary to add water to make up the quantity.

Sprinkle the gelatin over the cold water. Let stand briefly to soften, then combine with the berry juice and the orange juice in a small saucepan. Heat gently over low heat until all the gelatin has liquefied. Allow to cool and set just to the consistency of egg white.

Arrange the remaining berries on top of the cake and spoon the gelatin mixture evenly over them. Chill the cake for 3 to 4 hours to set the gelatin. At serving time, remove the sides of the pan and clean up any dribbles.

Yields 12 rich servings.

## Cranberry Glazed Cheesecake

A more modest cheesecake — but only in size. Cranberries provide the perfect contrast in colour and tartness to the richness of the filling.

CRUST:
1 cup (250 mL) sifted all-
   purpose flour
3 Tbs (45 mL) granulated sugar
¼ tsp (1 mL) salt
½ cup (125 mL) butter
½ tsp (3 mL) grated orange or
   lemon rind
1 egg yolk

FILLING:
12 oz (375 g) cream cheese, at
   room temperature
¾ tsp (4 mL) vanilla
pinch of salt
2 eggs
½ cup (125 mL) granulated sugar

GLAZE:
1 cup (250 mL) granulated sugar
1 Tbs (15 mL) cornstarch
⅔ cup (150 mL) water
2 cups (500 mL) cranberries
¼ tsp (1 mL) almond extract
(optional)

Lightly butter the bottom and sides of a 9" (3 L) spring-form pan. Preheat oven to 350°F (180°C).

To make the crust, combine the flour, sugar and salt in a large bowl. Cut in the butter, working until the mixture has the consistency of rolled oats. Add the rind. Beat the yolk lightly and drizzle over the other ingredients. Stir and toss thoroughly. This forms not a dough, but rather rough crumbs that stick together when baked. Press evenly over the bottom and about 1" (2.5 cm) up the sides of the pan. Bake the crust for 18 to 20 minutes, or until lightly browned.

Meanwhile, prepare the filling. Beat the cheese, vanilla and salt together until fluffy. In a separate bowl beat the eggs and sugar until light and lemon-coloured. Beat gradually into the cream cheese. Spread over the baked shell. Bake for 20 to 25 minutes more, or until just set, but still soft in the middle. Cool completely and chill.

To prepare the glaze, pour the sugar into a medium saucepan and blend in the cornstarch, then the water. Bring to the boil over high heat, then reduce the heat and cook 2 to 3 minutes, or until the sauce thickens and clears. Add the berries, bring back to the boil, then adjust the heat so that the berries bubble and seethe. Stir periodically to prevent sticking but be careful not to break up the berries. Remove from the heat after about 4 to 5 minutes, when the berries have popped and the sauce has thickened and turned a gorgeous red. Add the almond extract. Cool completely.

Spread over the chilled cheesecake. Refrigerate a minimum of 1 hour before removing the sides of the spring-form pan to serve.

Yields 8 to 10 servings.

# Blueberry Upside-Down Cake

Upside-down cakes reached a zenith of popularity in the 1940s. They have the advantage of good looks — especially when the fruit is carefully arranged — and adaptability. Served warm from the oven, they are puddings; when cooled and turned out, cakes glistening with fruit. A bowl of whipped cream or sour cream goes well with either the warm or cooled versions.

FRUIT LAYER:
3 Tbs (45 mL) butter
⅓ cup (75 mL) firmly packed brown sugar
2 cups (500 mL) blueberries
½ tsp (3 mL) grated lemon rind
2 tsp (10 mL) lemon juice

BATTER:
½ cup (125 mL) butter
¾ cup (175 mL) firmly packed brown sugar
1 egg
1 tsp (5 mL) vanilla
1⅓ cups (325 mL) sifted all-purpose flour
2 tsp (10 mL) baking powder
¼ tsp (1 mL) salt
1 tsp (5 mL) cinnamon
⅛ tsp (0.5 mL) ground cloves
¾ cup (175 mL) milk

Preheat oven to 375°F (190°C).

To make the fruit layer, melt the butter in a 9" x 9" (2.5 L) cake pan. Remove from the heat. Using a pastry brush or a piece of wax paper, grease the sides of the pan with some of the melted butter. Spread the brown sugar and then the blueberries evenly in the pan. Sprinkle on the rind and juice. Reserve.

To make the batter, cream the butter, add the brown sugar and beat until smooth and creamy. Blend in the egg and vanilla.

Sift the dry ingredients together. Add to the batter in 3 portions, alternately with the milk, in 2 portions. Spoon evenly over the fruit layer.

Bake for 40 to 50 minutes, or until a skewer inserted in the middle comes out clean. Let stand 10 minutes in the pan and then turn out onto a large flat serving plate.

Serve while still warm, with a bowl of lightly whipped cream, sour cream or yogurt.

Yields about 9 servings.

# Rhubarb Upside-Down Cake

FRUIT LAYER:
3 Tbs (50 mL) butter
3½ cups (875 mL) rhubarb, in 2"
 (5 cm) pieces
¾ cup (175 mL) granulated sugar
¼ tsp (1 mL) cinnamon

BATTER:
See Blueberry Upside-Down
 Cake (above)

Preheat oven to 375°F (190°C).

To make the fruit layer, place the butter in a 9" x 9" (2.5 L) cake pan and set in the oven just long enough to melt it. Brush the sides of the pan with some of the melted butter. Arrange the rhubarb, flat side down, in 4 even rows in the pan. Sprinkle the sugar and the cinnamon over the fruit, cover with aluminum foil and bake 10 minutes. Remove the foil.

Prepare the batter and bake the cake according to the instructions for the Blueberry Upside-Down Cake. To serve, cut the cake along the rows of rhubarb.

Yields about 9 servings.

# Upside-Down Cranberry Nut Cake

FRUIT LAYER:
2 Tbs (30 mL) butter
1½ cups (375 mL) cranberries
⅓ cup (75 mL) blanched slivered
  almonds
⅓ cup (75 mL) firmly packed
  brown sugar
2 tsp (10 mL) grated orange rind

BATTER:
1 egg
½ tsp (3 mL) vanilla
⅛ tsp (0.5 mL) salt
½ cup (125 mL) firmly packed
  brown sugar
½ cup (125 mL) sifted all-
  purpose flour
⅓ cup (75 mL) butter, melted
  and cooled

Preheat oven to 325°F (160°C).

To make the fruit layer, melt the butter in an 8" x 8" (2 L) cake tin. Using a pastry brush or piece of wax paper, grease the sides of the pan with some of the melted butter. Combine the cranberries, almonds, sugar and rind; spread evenly in the pan.

To make the batter, beat the egg until foamy, then beat in the vanilla, salt and brown sugar. Gradually stir in the flour, then the melted butter. Spoon evenly over the fruit layer. There will be just enough batter to go over the berries.

Bake for 40 to 45 minutes, or until a skewer inserted into the batter comes out clean. The berries will have bubbled up around the sides.

Immediately run a knife around the sides of the cake, place a large serving plate over the cake tin and invert to turn it out. Pour any butter remaining in the pan over the cranberries.

This is good served warm, with lightly whipped cream or good vanilla ice cream, or served cold, with sour cream.

Yields 8 generous servings.

# Raspberry Filbert Meringue Torte

MERINGUE:
pinch of salt
pinch of cream of tartar
4 egg whites at room temperature
1 cup (250 mL) granulated sugar
1 tsp (5 mL) vanilla
½ cup (125 mL) ground filberts
½ cup (125 mL) unblanched
  ground almonds

FILLING AND ICING:
2 cups (500 mL) heavy cream
⅓ cup (75 mL) sifted icing sugar
½ tsp (3 mL) vanilla
1 tsp (5 mL) unflavoured gelatin
1 Tbs (15 mL) water
1 cup (250 mL) raspberries,
  blueberries, blackberries or
  hulled sliced strawberries
⅓ cup (75 mL) finely chopped
  filberts

Butter two 8" (1.2 L) layer pans. Dust with flour and line with circles of parchment or wax paper cut to fit. Preheat oven to 350°F (180°C).

To prepare the meringue, sprinkle the salt and cream of tartar over the egg whites. Beat at low speed until foamy, then increase the speed to high and beat to soft peaks. Still beating, add the sugar gradually and continue beating until the meringue stands in firm peaks. Fold in the vanilla and the nuts.

Scrape the meringue into the prepared pans. Smooth the tops with a spatula and bake for 30 to 35 minutes, or until evenly browned.

Remove the layers from the pans and cool thoroughly on racks. Peel off the paper. The cakes can be made three or four days in advance and stored in an airtight container.

For the filling, whip the cream to firm peaks. Sweeten and flavour. Scoop out about half and reserve in the refrigerator. Combine the gelatin and water in a small saucepan; heat gently just long enough to dissolve the gelatin. Mix into the cream. Fold in the fruit.

Spread the whipped cream-fruit mixture over one layer of the cake. Position the other layer over the filling. Ice the cake with the remaining cream and sprinkle the filberts over the top. Transfer to a serving plate and chill.

Yields 8 to 10 luscious servings.

# Strawberry Shortcake

Before widespread refrigeration, sour cream was a frequent ingredient in baked goods. And a good thing! It makes the biscuits for these traditional shortcakes particularly light and tender. Raspberries and blackberries make good shortcake too.

1½ cups (375 mL) hulled sliced
   strawberries
3 Tbs (45 mL) granulated sugar
6 warm Sour Cream Shortcake
   Biscuits (below)

1 cup (250 mL) heavy cream
1 Tbs (15 mL) soft butter
6 perfect hulled strawberries

Combine the sliced berries and sugar in a bowl; cover and let stand 1 hour at room temperature.

Prepare the biscuits. While they are cooling, whip the cream. Split six of the still warm biscuits, butter both halves of each one and position the bottom halves in individual serving dishes. Spoon about ¼ cup (60 mL) of the sliced berries into each dish, put the biscuit top back on and slather with whipped cream. Set a strawberry, tip up, in the cream and serve right away.

Yields 6 servings.

# Sour Cream Shortcake Biscuits

2 cups (500 mL) sifted all-
purpose flour
2 Tbs (30 mL) granulated sugar
1 Tbs (15 mL) baking powder
½ tsp (3 mL) baking soda
½ tsp (3 mL) salt
3 Tbs (45 mL) cold butter

1 egg
1 cup (250 mL) sour cream

GLAZE:
2 Tbs (25 mL) light cream
2 Tbs (25 mL) granulated sugar

Dust a large baking sheet lightly with flour. Preheat the oven to 450°F (230°C).

Sift the first 5 ingredients into a large bowl. Using a pastry blender or 2 knives, cut the butter into the dry ingredients. Beat the egg lightly, mix into the sour cream, then pour all this over the dry ingredients. Blend together briefly using a fork.

Form into a ball and place on a floured counter. Roll out to ¾" (2 cm) and cut out about ten 2½" (6 cm) biscuits.

Place on the baking sheet, brush the tops with the light cream and sprinkle on the sugar for the glaze. Bake for 15 minutes or until well risen and brown.

Yields about 10 biscuits — enough for shortcake for six and a breakfast treat.

# Raspberry Filbert Meringue Bars

One of the very best bar cookies, with a layer of rich shortbread, then tart crunchy raspberry jam in the middle and a nutty meringue topping.

BASE:
½ cup (125 mL) butter
½ cup (125 mL) icing sugar
2 egg yolks
1¼ cups (300 mL) sifted all-purpose flour

TOPPING:
2 egg whites
pinch of salt

pinch of cream of tartar
½ cup (125 mL) granulated sugar
1 cup (250 mL) ground filberts
or blanched ground almonds
1 tsp (5 mL) vanilla (for the filberts) or ½ tsp (3 mL) almond extract (for the almonds)
¾ cup (175 mL) raspberry jam or jelly (see Preserving chapter)

Butter a 9" x 9" (2.5 L) cake tin. Preheat oven to 350°F (180°C).

To make the base, cream the butter, then beat in the icing sugar and the egg yolks, one at a time. Continue beating until the mixture is light and fluffy. Gradually blend in the flour. Press this pastry into the bottom of the cake tin. Bake for 15 to 18 minutes, or until very lightly browned. Remove from the oven and cool 5 minutes.

In the meantime, prepare the topping. Place the egg whites in a large bowl and sprinkle on the salt and cream of tartar. Beat slowly until frothy, then increase the speed to high and beat until soft peaks form. Gradually beat in the sugar, continuing until the meringue forms firm glossy peaks. Fold in the nuts and flavouring.

Very carefully spread an even layer of jam over the base, then an even layer of the meringue over the jam. Run a fork over the surface to create a pattern.

Bake 25 to 30 minutes more, or until the top is set and lightly browned. Cool and cut. Store, if desired, in an airtight container.

Yields 24 bars.

# Cocoanut Raspberry Jam Bars

Substitute shredded cocoanut for the nuts in the topping of Raspberry Filbert Meringue Bars. Flavour with vanilla.

# Many-Berry Muffins

It's a good idea to have a basic recipe to vary according to the availability of berries. To dress up these muffins, spoon 1 Tbs (15 mL) of the topping from Blueberry Buckle (page 36) over each tin of batter before popping the muffins into the oven.

3 cups (750 mL) sifted all-purpose flour
⅓ cup (75 mL) granulated sugar
1 Tbs (15 mL) baking powder
1 tsp (5 mL) salt
½ cup (125 mL) firmly packed brown sugar

3 eggs
½ cup (125 mL) butter, melted and cooled
1 cup (250 mL) milk
1 cup (250 mL) halved strawberries, whole blueberries, raspberries or saskatoons

Butter 15 large muffin tins. Reserve. Preheat oven to 400°F (200°C).

Sift the first 4 ingredients together into a large bowl. Add the brown sugar, mashing and stirring to blend it in with the other dry ingredients.

In a smaller bowl, beat the eggs, then add the butter and milk. Pour over the dry ingredients, sprinkle the fruit over the top and stir briefly, just enough to blend dry, liquid and fruit. Spoon into the muffin tins.

Bake for 20 minutes, or until the muffins are brown and spring back when lightly touched. Remove from the tins and cool on a rack.

Yields 15 large muffins.

# Berry Layer Muffins

My favourite variant for this recipe is not a berry at all but stemmed red currants. Try these muffins when the bush in the garden hasn't yielded enough for jelly or a pie.

BATTER:
⅓ cup (75 mL) butter
⅔ cup (150 mL) firmly packed
   brown sugar
2 eggs
¾ cup (175 mL) milk
½ tsp (3 mL) vanilla
2 cups (500 mL) sifted all-
   purpose flour
4 tsp (20 mL) baking powder
½ tsp (3 mL) salt

FILLING:
¾ cup (175 mL) fresh whole
   cranberries, blueberries,
   raspberries, saskatoons,
   stemmed red currants, hulled
   halved strawberries, or a thick
   cranberry sauce

TOPPING:
2 Tbs (25 mL) granulated sugar
1 tsp (5 mL) cinnamon

Butter 12 large muffin tins. Reserve. Preheat oven to 375°F (190°C).

To make the batter, cream together the butter and brown sugar until fluffy. Beat in the eggs, milk and vanilla. Don't be alarmed if the mixture curdles.

Sift together the flour, baking powder and salt. Add all at once to the creamed mixture and stir very briefly, just enough to dampen the dry ingredients. Don't try to beat out the lumps.

Fill the muffin tins halfway with this batter. Place a heaping spoonful of fruit or sauce filling in the centre of the batter and fill the tins with the remaining batter.

For the topping, combine the sugar and cinnamon and sprinkle evenly over the top of the batter.

Bake for 20 to 25 minutes, or until well risen and browned. Remove from the tins and cool on a rack.

Yields 12 large muffins.

# Blueberry Bran Muffins

1 cup (250 mL) bran
1 cup (250 mL) milk
¼ cup (50 mL) brown sugar
1 egg
¼ cup (50 mL) butter, melted
and cooled
1 tsp (5 mL) grated orange rind

1¼ cups (300 mL) sifted all-
purpose flour
4 tsp (20 mL) baking powder
½ tsp (3 mL) salt
¾ cup (175 mL) blueberries or
saskatoons

Butter 12 large muffin tins. Preheat oven to 400°F (200°C).

Combine the bran, milk and brown sugar in a large bowl. Let stand 10 minutes to allow the bran to absorb the milk. Add the egg, butter and orange rind. Beat well.

Sift together the flour, baking powder and salt. Combine with the berries and pour this mixture over the bran. Stir briskly, just long enough to mix the liquid and dry ingredients.

Spoon into the muffin tins and bake for 20 minutes. The muffins will be browned and spring back when lightly touched. Remove from the tins and cool on a rack.

Yields 12 muffins.

# Cranberry Lemon Muffins

Every year muffins get more and more popular. They are one of the first things children learn how to make at school, and they remain one of the most easily whipped-up treats in the kitchen.

1¾ cups (425 mL) cranberries
2 cups (500 mL) sifted all-
  purpose flour
1 Tbs (15 mL) baking powder
½ tsp (3 mL) salt
¾ cup (175 mL) firmly packed
  brown sugar

1 egg
¼ cup (60 mL) butter, melted
  and cooled
1 cup (250 mL) milk
1½ tsp (8 mL) grated lemon rind
freshly grated nutmeg

Grease 12 large muffin tins. Reserve. Preheat oven to 400°F (200°C). Toss the cranberries with ¼ cup (50 mL) of the flour; set aside.
  Sift the remaining flour, baking powder and salt into a large bowl. Blend the brown sugar into the dry ingredients.
  In a smaller bowl, beat the egg lightly, mix in the butter, milk and lemon rind and pour over the sifted dry ingredients. Sprinkle the berries over the top and stir just enough to incorporate the wet into the dry. Spoon into the muffin tins. Dust lightly with nutmeg.
  Bake for 20 minutes, or until the muffins are evenly browned and firm to the touch. Remove from the tins and cool on a rack.

Yields 12 big muffins.

# Classic Cranberry Orange Nut Loaf

BATTER:
2 cups (500 mL) sifted all-
  purpose flour
1 cup (250 mL) granulated sugar
1½ tsp (8 mL) baking powder
½ tsp (3 mL) baking soda
½ tsp (3 mL) salt
⅓ cup (75 mL) butter or shortening
1 cup (250 mL) coarsely
  chopped cranberries

½ cup (125 mL) coarsely
  chopped fresh walnuts,
  pecans or almonds
1 Tbs (15 mL) grated orange rind
1 egg
¾ cup (200 mL)  orange juice

TOPPING:
2 Tbs (25 mL) icing sugar

Butter and lightly flour a 9" x 5" (2 L) loaf tin. Preheat oven to 350°F (180°C).

Sift the first 5 ingredients together into a large bowl. Cut the butter in until the mixture is crumbly. Add the cranberries, nuts and orange rind. Mix well to disperse the berries and nuts.

Beat the egg and the orange juice together. Pour over the dry ingredients and mix just enough to blend.

Turn into the tin, spreading batter evenly, and bake for 1 hour, or until a skewer inserted in the middle comes out clean. Cool 10 minutes in the tin, then turn out onto a rack and cool thoroughly. Wrap well and store in an airtight container for a day. Before slicing, sift the icing sugar over the top of the loaf. Yields 1 loaf.

## Cranberry Whole-Wheat Loaf

This loaf has the fragrance of good whole-wheat flour and wheat germ.

2 cups (500 mL) whole-wheat flour
½ cup (125 mL) wheat germ
1 cup (250 mL) firmly packed brown sugar
1 tsp (5 mL) salt
2 tsp (10 mL) baking powder
½ tsp (3 mL) baking soda
1½ cups (375 mL) halved cranberries
½ cup (125 mL) chopped fresh walnuts
1 egg
1 Tbs (15 mL) grated orange rind
¼ cup (60 mL) oil
¾ cup (175 mL) orange juice
2 Tbs (25 mL) sesame seeds (optional)

Butter and lightly flour a 9" x 5" (2 L) loaf tin. Preheat oven to 350°F (180°C).

Blend the first 6 ingredients thoroughly in a large bowl. Sprinkle 2 Tbs (25 mL) of this mixture over the cranberries and walnuts and toss together lightly.

Break the egg into a medium bowl. Beat together with the orange rind, oil and juice. Pour evenly over the top of the whole-wheat mixture. Using a fork, mix just enough to blend dry and liquid. Add the dredged fruit and nuts; mix briefly.

Turn into the prepared tin, spreading batter evenly, and sprinkle on the sesame seeds. Press seeds down very lightly.

Bake for 50 to 60 minutes, or until a skewer inserted in the middle comes out clean. Cool 10 minutes in the pan, then turn out onto a rack. Wrap well and store in an airtight container for a day before using. Cut into ½" (12 mm) slices. Yields 1 loaf.

# Blueberry Buttermilk Loaf

It's important to dredge the berries to spread them evenly through this moist, mildly aromatic loaf.

2 eggs
1 cup (250 mL) buttermilk
1 tsp (5 mL) vanilla
6 Tbs (100 mL) butter, melted
  and cooled
½ cup (125 mL) firmly packed
  brown sugar
1 cup (250 mL) rolled oats
2 cups (500 mL) sifted all-
  purpose flour

2 tsp (10 mL) baking powder
1 tsp (5 mL) baking soda
½ tsp (3 mL) salt
½ tsp (3 mL) cardamom
½ tsp (3 mL) freshly grated
  nutmeg
1 cup (250 mL) blueberries
½ cup (125 mL) finely chopped
  almonds, pecans or
  fresh walnuts

Butter and lightly flour a 9" x 5" (2 L) loaf pan. Preheat oven to 350°F (180°C).

Break the eggs into a medium-large bowl. Beat until frothy with the buttermilk, vanilla and butter. Stir in the brown sugar and rolled oats. Set aside while preparing the rest of the batter.

Sift together, into a large bowl, the flour, baking powder, soda, salt and spices. Sprinkle 2 Tbs (25 mL) of this mixture over the berries and nuts; toss lightly.

Pour the buttermilk mixture over the sifted dry ingredients. Using a fork, mix lightly and quickly, then blend in the dredged fruit and nuts.

Spread evenly in the loaf tin and bake for 1 hour, or until a skewer inserted in the middle comes out clean. Cool in the pan 10 minutes; turn out onto a rack to finish the cooling. Wrap well and store in an airtight container for a day before slicing.

Yields 1 loaf.

# Cranberry Pancakes

This basic pancake recipe can have any berry in it, but increase the quantity of the sweeter ones like strawberries, blueberries, blackberries or raspberries (see below). The strawberry version is good with sour cream and brown sugar.

2 cups (500 mL) sifted all-purpose flour
⅓ cup (75 mL) granulated sugar
4 tsp (20 mL) baking powder
½ tsp (3 mL) salt
2 eggs

1¾ cups (450 mL) milk
¼ cup (50 mL) butter, melted and cooled
1 cup (250 mL) roughly chopped cranberries

Sift all the dry ingredients together into a large bowl.

Break the eggs into a medium bowl; beat lightly. Blend in the milk and butter. Pour over the dry mixture, add the cranberries and mix just enough to blend the dry and liquid ingredients.

Lightly grease a griddle or frying pan. Heat to medium-high and pour in the batter, about ¼ cup (50 mL) for each pancake. Cook until the top of the pancake is covered with bubbles and the edges begin to lose their shine. Turn and cook briefly on the other side, just long enough to brown. Serve with butter and maple syrup.

For other berries — blueberries, saskatoons, raspberries, blackberries and strawberries — increase the quantity of berries to 1½ cups (375 mL) and decrease the sugar to 3 Tbs (45 mL).

Yields 6 servings.

# Blueberry Buttermilk Pancakes

This is a standard buttermilk pancake recipe that can be varied with any sweet berry or even ½ cup (125 mL) well-drained Baked Spring Rhubarb (page 70). The batter is somewhat stiff but makes the lightest possible pancakes. Note that these pancakes cook at a lower temperature than most.

2 cups (500 mL) sifted all-
  purpose flour
2 Tbs (25 mL) granulated sugar
2 tsp (10 mL) baking powder
1 tsp (5 mL) baking soda
½ tsp (3 mL) salt
¼ tsp (1 mL) freshly grated
  nutmeg
2 eggs

2 cups (500 mL) buttermilk
¼ cup (50 mL) butter, melted
  and cooled
¼ tsp (1 mL) grated orange or
  lemon rind
1 cup (250 mL) blueberries,
  saskatoons, raspberries or
  hulled halved strawberries

Sift all the dry ingredients together into a large bowl.

Break the eggs into a medium bowl, beat lightly and mix in the buttermilk, melted butter and rind. Pour over the dry ingredients, add the berries and mix just enough to blend. Cook on a lightly greased griddle or frying pan at medium-low heat, allowing about ¼ cup (50 mL) batter for each 4″ (10 cm) pancake. Turn each pancake when the top is covered with bubbles and the edges begin to lose their shine. Cook until golden brown.

Serve with butter and syrup — try blueberry syrup with these pancakes.

Yields 5 to 6 servings.


# Fresh Strawberry Crêpes

12 crêpes (see below)
3 cups (750 mL) hulled sliced
  strawberries
⅓ cup (75 mL) granulated sugar
1 Tbs (15 mL) framboise, kirsch,

strawberry or orange liqueur
  (optional)
1 cup (250 mL) heavy cream
12 perfect small unhulled
  strawberries

Prepare the crêpes.

Combine the sliced berries, sugar and liqueur in a bowl. Toss lightly, cover and let stand an hour or so at room temperature. Stir again.

To serve, whip the cream. Spread about ¼ cup (60 mL) sliced berries and juice over each crêpe, roll up loosely and place 2 crêpes on each plate. Pipe a rosette or spoon a dab of the whipped cream onto each crêpe and place an unhulled berry, tip down, in each rosette. Serve immediately.

Yields 6 servings (allowing 2 crêpes per person).

## Crêpes

1 cup (250 mL) sifted all-purpose flour
⅓ cup (75 mL) icing sugar
pinch of salt
3 eggs

1½ cups (375 mL) milk
1 Tbs (15 mL) butter, melted and cooled
melted butter or oil

The easiest way to make crêpes is to combine all the ingredients in a blender or food processor and whirl 30 seconds. Stop the machine, scrape down the sides and whirl again long enough to make a smooth batter.

Otherwise, mix the flour, icing sugar and salt in a large bowl. In a smaller bowl beat together the eggs, milk and butter; pour these liquid ingredients over the dry and beat until the batter is smooth and has the consistency of thick cream.

Cover and refrigerate the batter 2 to 24 hours before making the crêpes.

To make the crêpes, heat a 6" (15 cm) crêpe pan or frying pan until a drop of water sizzles and bounces on it. Using a pastry brush, very lightly brush the surface of the pan with either melted butter or oil. Pour in about 3 Tbs (45 mL) crêpe batter, lift the pan off the heat and rotate it rapidly to spread the batter over the entire bottom surface. Return to the heat. Cook for about 30 seconds, or until the top of the crêpe has lost its shininess and the bottom is browned. Loosen an edge, flip over and cook the other side for 10 to 15 seconds. Remove from the pan and cool on towelling. Continue with the remaining batter.

This recipe yields about 20 crêpes. To store the extra crêpes for another occasion, stack them up on a large piece of aluminum foil, separated by squares of wax paper. Fold the ends of the foil over and pinch the edges to make an airtight package. Refrigerate for up to 2 days, or freeze for longer storage.

# Strawberry Ice Cream Crêpes

Proceed as for Fresh Strawberry Crêpes, but fill each crêpe with softened good vanilla ice cream and use the sweetened sliced berries for a topping. Allow ⅓ to ½ cup (75 to 125 mL) ice cream per crêpe.

# Blueberry Crêpes

Fill crêpes with whipped cream or ice cream and cover with Blueberry Sauce (page 74).

# Raspberry Crêpes

Fill crêpes with whipped cream or ice cream and cover with Fresh Raspberry Sauce (page 76).

# COLD DESSERTS, SAUCES, SHERBETS, ICE CREAMS AND HOT PUDDINGS

## Strawberry Fool

A fool is one of the simplest but most delicious of summer fruit desserts. Basically, it is whipped cream blended into puréed fruit.

5 cups (1.25 L) hulled strawberries
1 cup (250 mL) granulated sugar
1 tsp (5 mL) brandy or light rum
   (optional)
1 cup (250 mL) heavy cream
6 sprigs fresh mint leaves

Reserve 6 perfect berries. Crush or purée the remaining berries using a coarse sieve, the medium disk of a food mill or a food processor, using the steel blade.

Combine the purée, sugar and brandy; let stand 1 hour at room temperature. Stir periodically to dissolve the sugar. Cover and chill.

Whip the cream and fold gently into the purée. Turn into a serving bowl or 6 individual bowls. Glass dishes show off the colour of the fool best. Decorate with a whole berry and a sprig of mint.

Yields 6 servings.

# Black Raspberry and Ginger Cream

Use any of the sweet black raspberries, black caps, blackberries or red raspberries for this variation on a fool. In the winter, substitute unsweetened frozen berries, partially thawed. To sift the brown sugar, press it through a coarse sieve and spoon into the measuring cup without packing it down.

5 cups (1.25 L) black raspberries
1½ cups (375 mL) heavy cream
½ cup (125 mL) sifted dark
  brown sugar
¼ tsp (2 mL) ground ginger
  or 2 tsp (10 mL) finely chopped
  crystallized or drained
  preserved ginger

GARNISH:
½ cup (125 mL) heavy cream
16 slivers of crystallized or
  drained preserved ginger

Put aside 16 perfect berries.

Whip the cream until stiff. Fold in the brown sugar, ginger and the rest of the berries. Turn into a large glass serving bowl or 8 individual dishes. Smooth the top. Cover and chill 2 hours.

To garnish, whip the remaining cream and pipe rosettes around the edge and in the middle of the large bowl or in the middle only of the individual dishes. Centre the raspberries in the rosettes and stick the ginger slivers into the cream next to them.

Yields 8 servings.

# Black Currant and Honey Fool

Use mild clover honey, liquid is easiest, to sweeten this fool.

2 cups (500 mL) black currants
½ cup (125 mL) liquid clover
  honey
1½ cups (375 mL) heavy cream

Combine the currants and honey in a heavy-bottomed saucepan. Cover, place over low heat and simmer gently, stirring frequently, until the currants are very tender, about 20 minutes. Pass through a food mill, using a fine disk, or press through a medium sieve. Cool thoroughly.

To serve, whip the cream and fold two-thirds of it gently into the fruit purée, leaving some distinct swirls of cream and currants. Spoon into a glass serving dish or 4 to 6 individual dishes. Pipe or spoon the remaining whipped cream over the fool.

Yields 4 to 6 servings.

# Rhubarb Fool

An excellent dessert for late winter, when the first hothouse rhubarb appears on the market. This forced rhubarb has a mild flavour and a particularly pink colour that looks attractive swirled through the whipped cream. But don't neglect this dessert during garden rhubarb time. Just use the pinkest and most tender stalks.

| | |
|---|---|
| 4 cups (1 L) finely chopped rhubarb, in ½″ (12 mm) pieces | 1 Tbs (15 mL) orange juice |
| 1 tsp (5 mL) grated orange rind | 1 cup (250 mL) granulated sugar |
| | 1 cup (250 mL) heavy cream |

Place the rhubarb, orange rind and juice in a heavy-bottomed saucepan over low heat. Cover and cook 20 to 25 minutes, or until the fruit is tender. Stir periodically and watch carefully, especially at the beginning, to prevent burning.

Add the sugar; stir and cook just long enough to dissolve the sugar. Blend, process or pass through a food mill. Cool, cover and chill the rhubarb thoroughly. This step can be done two or three days before serving.

Just before serving, whip the cream. Fold in the chilled rhubarb purée, leaving swirled traces of cream and rhubarb. Pour into a crystal or glass bowl.

Yields 6 servings.

# Strawberry Sherry Trifle

Vary the fruit according to what's available — strawberries in the spring, red or black raspberries or blueberries in the summer. Recipes for suitable jams can be found in the chapter on preserves, but don't neglect the possibility of using Red Currant Jelly (page 105), especially with blueberries.

two 8″ (1.2 L) Hot Milk Sponge Cake layers (below)

1 recipe Rich Custard Sauce (below)
6 Tbs (100 mL) sherry
6 Tbs (100 mL) strawberry jam

2 cups (500 mL) hulled sliced strawberries
¾ cup (175 mL) heavy cream
2 cups (500 mL) hulled strawberries

Prepare the cake and custard sauce. If necessary, trim around the sponge layers to fit neatly into the serving bowl. Slice each layer horizontally with a serrated knife to make 4 thin layers.

Place one layer in the bottom of the bowl. Sprinkle with a quarter of the sherry. Spread a third of the jam evenly over the cake and spoon in a third of the custard, then a third of the sliced berries. Continue with more layers of cake, sherry, jam, custard and berries, ending with the fourth sponge layer and the final sprinkle of sherry. Cover with plastic wrap and chill at least 4 hours, but preferably overnight.

To serve, whip the cream and spread evenly over the top. Stud with the whole berries, tips up.

Yields 10 generous servings.

# Hot Milk Sponge Cake

1 cup (250 mL) sifted all-purpose flour
1 tsp (5 mL) baking powder
2 eggs
¼ tsp (1 mL) salt

¾ cup (175 mL) granulated sugar
1 tsp (5 mL) vanilla
½ tsp (3 mL) grated orange rind
½ cup (125 mL) milk
1 Tbs (15 mL) butter

Prepare two 8" (1.2 L) layer cake tins by cutting two disks of wax paper to fit into them. Preheat oven to 350°F (180°C). (No greasing is needed for sponge cakes!)

Sift the flour and baking powder together twice. Separate the eggs, dropping the whites into a large bowl and the yolks into a small bowl.

Sprinkle the salt over the whites; beat at low speed until frothy. Increase the speed to high and beat to soft peaks. Gradually add ¼ cup (50 mL) of the sugar while continuing to beat to a firm, glossy meringue.

Pour the remaining sugar, the vanilla and the orange rind onto the yolks; beat until the mixture is straw-coloured and ribbony.

Heat the milk and butter together until the butter has melted and the milk is heated through — steaming but not boiling. Fold the yolk mixture into the whites, then the sifted dry ingredients, a third at a time. Finally fold the hot liquid into the batter.

Scrape the batter into the prepared pans, smooth out the tops and bake for 25 minutes, or until the cake springs back when lightly pressed. Cool 10 minutes in the pans; run a knife around the edge of the cakes, invert gently and cool on racks.

The cake can be made a day before assembling the trifle. Store the layers in an airtight container. It can also be frozen, wrapped well in an airtight container.

## Rich Custard Sauce

2 cups (500 mL) light cream or
   milk
¼ cup (50 mL) granulated sugar

¼ tsp (1 mL) salt
½ tsp (3 mL) grated orange rind
5 egg yolks or 3 eggs

Combine the cream, sugar, salt and orange rind in the top of a double boiler and heat to scalding point over direct medium heat.

Whisk the egg yolks or eggs. Pour about a quarter of the hot cream onto the eggs, whisking all the time, then pour back into the rest of the cream, continuing to whisk. Place over simmering water and cook, stirring constantly, until the mixture is thick enough to coat a spoon, about 4 to 5 minutes. This usually happens at 165°F (74°C).

Cool, whisking periodically to prevent a skin from forming on the top.

# Victorian Vanilla Cream

1 Tbs (15 mL) unflavoured gelatin
¼ cup (50 mL) cold water
3 eggs
½ cup (125 mL) granulated sugar
1 cup (250 mL) milk

1 tsp (5 mL) vanilla
pinch of salt
pinch of cream of tartar
1 cup (250 mL) heavy cream

Lightly oil a 6 cup (1.5 L) mould.

Stir the gelatin into the water; let stand to soften. Separate the eggs, dropping the whites into a large bowl and the yolks into a small one. Reserve the whites at room temperature.

Beat the yolks with half the sugar. Scald the milk in the top of a double boiler, directly over medium heat, and blend into the yolks. Pour this mixture back into the double boiler and set over simmering water. Stir and cook about 4 to 8 minutes, or until thickened enough to coat a spoon, at about 165°F (74°C).

Remove from the heat. Stir in the softened gelatin, mixing until all granules have dissolved, then add the vanilla. Strain into a medium bowl. Cool and chill, whisking periodically, until partially set, about 45 minutes.

Sprinkle the salt and cream of tartar over the egg whites. Beat until foamy at low speed, then increase speed to high and beat to soft peaks. Continue beating, while adding the remaining sugar, until the meringue is firm.

Whip the cream. Stir about a quarter of the meringue into the custard, fold in the whipped cream, then fold this mixture into the remaining egg whites. Scrape into the prepared mould or a glass bowl; cover and chill until set, at least 4 hours.

Unmould onto a serving dish and accompany with the Fresh Strawberry Sauce (page 77), Fresh Raspberry Sauce (page 76), any of the cranberry sauces (pages 74-76), or 2 to 3 cups (500 to 750 mL) fresh hulled sliced strawberries, whole raspberries or blueberries.

Yields 8 servings.

# Ripe Gooseberry Bavarian Cream

If you can't wait for your gooseberries to turn rosy, or if only green ones are available on the market, don't hesitate to make this cream. Add another ¼ cup (50 mL) granulated sugar to the gooseberry purée and expect a pale green Bavarian.

3 cups (750 mL) ripe
  gooseberries
½ cup (125 mL) water
1 cup (250 mL) granulated sugar
1 Tbs (15 mL) lemon juice
1 cup (250 mL) milk
¼ tsp (1 mL) salt
2 eggs, well beaten

½ tsp (3 mL) vanilla
1 Tbs (15 mL) unflavoured gelatin
2 Tbs (30 mL) orange juice
1½ cups (375 mL) heavy cream

GARNISH:
a few sprigs of mint, gooseberry
  leaves or elderberry flowers

Combine the gooseberries with the water in a saucepan. Cover and bring to the boil; then reduce heat to very low and simmer 5 minutes, or until the berries are tender. Press through a medium sieve or food mill, using a fine disk. Dissolve ½ cup (125 mL) of the sugar in the hot purée. Add the lemon juice, pour into a large bowl and reserve in the refrigerator.

Combine the milk, the remaining sugar and the salt in the top of a double boiler over direct medium heat; scald. Pour about a quarter of the hot milk onto the eggs, whisking continuously, then pour the mixture back into the top of the double boiler. Place over simmering water and cook until it reaches 165ºF (74ºC) or is thickened, about 5 minutes. Stir constantly to prevent curdling. Remove from the heat; add the vanilla.

Mix the gelatin into the orange juice and let soften. Add to the hot custard and stir until the granules have all dissolved. Cool, stirring periodically. Mix into the gooseberry purée. Refrigerate until partially set, about 1 hour.

Whip 1 cup (250 mL) of the cream and fold gently into the fruit mixture. Turn into a 6 cup (1.5 L) glass serving dish. Chill at least 4 hours. To serve, whip the remaining cream and spoon or pipe around the edges of the bowl as a garnish. Add a few sprigs of greenery.

Yields 8 generous servings.

# Cranberry Bavarian Cream

2½ cups (625 mL) cranberries
1 cup (250 mL) Cranberry Juice
  (page 111)
1 cup (250 mL) milk
¾ cup (175 mL) granulated sugar

4 eggs
1 Tbs (15 mL) unflavoured gelatin
pinch of salt
pinch of cream of tartar
1¼ cups (300 mL) heavy cream

Combine the cranberries and juice in a saucepan. Cover and bring to the boil over high heat; then reduce the heat and simmer gently until the berries are tender, about 8 to 10 minutes. Drain liquid into a medium bowl; reserve 15 of the best-looking berries for the garnish, and measure out ¼ cup (50 mL) of the liquid and reserve to soften the gelatin. Purée the berries through a sieve or a food mill fitted with a fine disk; discard the seeds and skins. Add to liquid and set aside to cool.

Combine the milk and all but 2 Tbs (25 mL) of the sugar in the top of a double boiler. Scald directly over medium heat. Separate the eggs, dropping the yolks into a medium bowl and the whites into a large bowl. Reserve the whites.

Beat the yolks briskly, pour the hot milk over them in a steady stream, beating constantly. Pour back into the top of the double boiler and place over simmering water. Cook and stir about 8 minutes, or until the custard reaches 165°F (74°C) or is thick enough to coat a wooden spoon. Remove from the heat.

Meanwhile, sprinkle the gelatin over the reserved cranberry juice, stir and let stand 2 to 3 minutes to soften. Stir into the hot custard until thoroughly dissolved. Pour the custard over the cranberry purée; mix and chill, stirring periodically, until thickened but not set, about 1½ hours.

Beat the egg whites, salt and cream of tartar at low speed until frothy. Beat at high speed to the soft peak stage, then gradually add the remaining 2 Tbs (25 mL) sugar and beat to the glossy firm peak stage. Whip ¾ cup (175 mL) of the cream.

Stir about a quarter of the egg whites into the cranberry custard, fold in the whipped cream, then pour this mixture over the whites and fold in thoroughly but gently. Turn into a large bowl, preferably glass, or individual glasses. Cover and chill until set, about 4 hours.

To assemble, whip the remaining cream and spoon 15 dabs or pipe 15 rosettes around the edge and centre of the bowl. Centre a cranberry on each rosette. Garnish individual glasses with whipped cream and berries. Yields 6 to 8 servings.

# White Wine Strawberry Mousse

The touches of ginger and white wine give a refreshing lightness to this easy dessert.

3 cups (750 mL) hulled
  strawberries
⅓ cup (75 mL) granulated sugar
½ cup (125 mL) white wine
4 tsp (20 mL) unflavoured gelatin
½ tsp (3 mL) grated lemon rind
1 tsp (5 mL) lemon juice
¼ tsp (1 mL) ground ginger
2 egg whites

pinch of salt
pinch of cream of tartar
¼ cup (50 mL) granulated sugar
1 cup (250 mL) heavy cream

GARNISH:
fresh mint leaves
6 perfect unhulled strawberries

Mash the strawberries thoroughly with a fork or purée in a food mill, using the coarse disk; in a blender; or in a food processor fitted with the steel blade, flicking on and off rapidly. There should be 1½ cups (375 mL) puréed berries. Place in a medium-large bowl; add the ⅓ cup (75 mL) sugar, cover and reserve.

Pour the wine into a small saucepan and stir in the gelatin. Place over low heat and cook, stirring, until the gelatin melts. Remove from the heat and add the lemon rind, juice and ginger. Mix with the berries and chill until partially set, about 1 hour.

Place the egg whites in a large bowl, sprinkle on the salt and cream of tartar and beat at low speed until foamy. Increase the speed to high and beat to soft peaks. Continue beating, while adding the remaining sugar, until the meringue stands in firm glossy peaks.

Whip the cream. Stir about a quarter of the whites into the strawberry mixture. Add the cream and fold in gently. Turn this mixture onto the remaining meringue and fold in thoroughly.

Spoon into a large bowl, preferably glass, and chill until firm, about 4 hours. Decorate the top with sprigs of fresh mint and unhulled berries.

Yields 6 servings.

# Classic Layered Strawberry Bavarian

A classic from a turn-of-the-century Ontario cookbook. Substitute raspberries after the strawberry season.

6 cups (1.5 L) hulled strawberries
1 cup (250 mL) granulated sugar
1 Tbs (15 mL) brandy, rum or
  orange liqueur
1 Tbs (15 mL) cornstarch
1½ cups (375 mL) milk
4 eggs

4½ tsp (25 mL) unflavoured
  gelatin
⅓ cup (75 mL) orange juice
pinch of salt
pinch of cream of tartar
1¼ cups (300 mL) heavy cream

Purée 2 cups (500 mL) of the berries using a coarse sieve, the medium disk of a food mill, a blender or a food processor fitted with the steel blade. Cover and refrigerate.

Slice the remaining berries in half lengthwise, into a medium bowl; sprinkle on 2 Tbs (25 mL) of the sugar and the brandy. Toss gently from time to time while proceeding with the other steps. Leave at room temperature.

Mix all but 2 Tbs (25 mL) of the remaining sugar with the cornstarch in the top of a double boiler. Blend in the milk. Set over direct medium heat and cook, stirring almost constantly, until slightly thickened. Reduce heat to low and simmer 8 minutes to cook the cornstarch.

Separate the eggs, dropping the yolks into a medium bowl and the whites into a large bowl. Reserve the whites at room temperature. Whisk the yolks, and while still whisking, pour in about a quarter of the hot milk mixture. Return this mixture to the top of the double boiler and place over simmering water. Continue cooking, stirring constantly, until the custard reaches 170°F (77°C) and thickens enough to coat a spoon, about 4 minutes. Remove from the heat.

Stir the gelatin into the orange juice, let stand briefly to soften the granules, then mix into the hot custard. Stir until the gelatin has completely dissolved. Cool the custard, stirring occasionally, and mix into the strawberry purée. Refrigerate until the mixture is partially set, about 1 hour.

Sprinkle the salt and cream of tartar over the egg whites, beat at low speed until frothy, then at high speed to soft peaks. Continue beating while adding the last of the sugar. The meringue is ready when it forms firm peaks. Whip ¾ cup (175 mL) of the cream.

To assemble the Bavarian, first drain the berries and mix the liquid into the partially set custard. Stir a quarter of the meringue into the custard, then fold in the whipped cream; pour this mixture over the remaining meringue and fold together gently but thoroughly.

Spread a third of the halved strawberries in the bottom of an 8 cup (2 L) glass bowl. Spoon in half the custard mixture, another third of the berries, then the remaining custard. Arrange the remaining berries, cut side down, in the centre of the bowl and around the edges. Cover and refrigerate until set, about 4 hours.

To serve, whip the remaining cream and pipe or spoon attractively between the berries at the edge and centre of the bowl.

Yields 8 to 10 servings.

## Strawberry Snow

2 cups (500 mL) hulled
  strawberries
2 egg whites
pinch of salt
pinch of cream of tartar

½ cup (125 mL) granulated sugar
2 cups (500 mL) hulled sliced or
  halved strawberries
1 recipe Rich Custard Sauce
  (page 61)

Purée the hulled berries using a coarse sieve or the medium disk of a food mill, or in a blender or a food processor fitted with the steel blade. Reserve.

Place the egg whites in a large bowl. Sprinkle on the salt and cream of tartar. Beat until foamy at low speed, increase the speed to high and beat to the soft peak stage. Add the sugar gradually, continuing to beat until the whites stand in firm glossy peaks. Still beating, add the puréed berries in a steady stream. Beat for about 5 more minutes. The berry meringue should be firm and voluminous. Turn into a glass serving bowl, cover and refrigerate until serving time. The snow holds its shape for up to 12 hours, but is best eaten within 2 hours.

At serving time, spoon a large dollop of the snow into individual dishes, add a portion of the sliced berries and pass the custard sauce.

Yields 6 servings.

# Raspberry Flummery

The layered look made it to cooking long before clothes, and no period had more layered puddings than the late nineteenth century. The raspberry layer at the bottom cooks just long enough to be juicy and fragrant.

CUSTARD:
¼ cup (50 mL) granulated sugar
1 Tbs (15 mL) cornstarch
pinch of salt
1 cup (250 mL) milk
1 cup (250 mL) light cream
3 egg yolks
½ tsp (3 mL) vanilla

MERINGUE:
3 egg whites, at room temperature
pinch of salt
pinch of cream of tartar
¼ cup (50 mL) granulated sugar

FRUIT:
3 cups (750 mL) raspberries
¼ cup (50 mL) granulated sugar

Preheat oven to 375°F (190°C).

To prepare the custard, combine the sugar, cornstarch and salt in the top of a double boiler. Stir in the milk and cream. Place directly over medium heat and cook until the mixture is slightly thickened and the taste of raw cornstarch is gone.

Beat the yolks in a bowl, pour in about half the hot milk mixture, mix well, and return all to the top of the double boiler. Place over simmering water. Stir all through this process. Cook the custard, continuing to stir, until it reaches 170°F (77°C), or is thick enough to coat a spoon, about 8 minutes. Remove from the heat, add the vanilla and reserve. Whisk once or twice.

To prepare the meringue, place the egg whites, salt and cream of tartar in a large bowl. Beat slowly until frothy, increase the speed to high and continue beating until the whites stand in soft peaks. Add the sugar gradually, continuing to beat until the whites stand in firm glossy peaks.

To assemble, place the raspberries in the bottom of an ovenproof 8 cup (2 L) dish, preferably glass. Sprinkle on the remaining sugar. Spoon the custard over the berries and finish with the meringue, swirling or piping it in a decorative pattern over the top.

Bake for 12 minutes, or until the swirls are a golden brown. Serve warm or chilled.

Yields 6 generous servings.

# Ruby Raspberry and Red Currant Mould

From a cookbook written in the 1880s, when packaged gelatin was an innovation.

2 cups (500 mL) stemmed red currants
¾ cup (175 mL) cold water
2⅓ cups (575 mL) raspberries

4 tsp (20 mL) unflavoured gelatin
1 cup (250 mL) granulated sugar
½ cup (125 mL) boiling water
1 cup (250 mL) heavy cream

Lightly oil a 4 cup (1 L) jelly mould.

Place the red currants and ½ cup (125 mL) of the water in a saucepan. Crush with a potato masher or mallet. Cover, bring to the boil, reduce heat immediately, and simmer 3 to 5 minutes, or until the currants are tender and their juice running; remove from the heat. Reserve ⅓ cup (75 mL) of the most perfect raspberries; add the rest to the currants and crush thoroughly. Wet a jelly bag, wring it out and pour the fruit and juice into it. Squeeze or press out all the juice. There should be about 2 cups (500 mL).

Stir the gelatin into the remaining water. Let stand a few minutes to soften. Combine the sugar and boiling water in a saucepan. Stir, bring to the boil, and boil vigorously for 2 minutes. Remove from the heat and add the gelatin mixture; stir until the gelatin has dissolved. Cool and combine with the fruit juice mixture.

Pour into the mould, cover and refrigerate until firm, a minimum of 4 hours. To unmould, cover with a flat serving plate, making sure that the mould is centred, and flip over together. Dip a clean towel in hot water, wring it out and wrap it loosely around the mould; leave it for a few seconds and the jelly should come out.

Whip the cream; pipe or spoon decoratively around the jelly. Garnish with the perfect berries. Keep chilled and serve within 2 hours.

Yields 6 servings.

# Baked Spring Rhubarb

Baking rhubarb is one good way to keep the pink rhubarb pieces from turning into a mass of fibres.

4 cups (1 L) chopped rhubarb, in
  1″ (2.5 cm) pieces
2″ (5 cm) piece cinnamon stick

1 cup (250 mL) granulated sugar
⅓ cup (75 mL) hot water

Preheat oven to 350°F (180°C).
  Place the rhubarb in a heatproof dish. Break the cinnamon into 4 pieces and nestle into the rhubarb. Mix the sugar and water together; pour over the rhubarb.
  Cover the dish and bake for 30 to 35 minutes, or until the rhubarb is tender. Uncover partially and cool. Remove the cinnamon. Store in the refrigerator.

Yields 6 generous servings.

# Summer Fruit Salad

Red currants are the unexpected touch in this fruit salad. Vary the berries according to availability.

½ cup (125 mL) granulated sugar
¾ cup (175 mL) white wine or
  water
3″ (7.5 cm) strip of orange peel
4 cups (1 L) peeled sliced peaches
1 cup (250 mL) stemmed red
  currants

2 cups (500 mL) blackberries or
  raspberries
1 cup (250 mL) blueberries
unsweetened whipped cream or
  Rich Custard Sauce (page 61)

Combine the sugar, wine and orange peel in a small saucepan. Bring to the boil over high heat, then reduce the heat and simmer gently 5 minutes. Cool and remove the orange peel.
  Place all the fruit in a large bowl and pour on the syrup; mix gently, cover and refrigerate 2 hours. Stir gently again.
  Serve in a glass bowl and pass the cream or sauce.

Yields 6 to 8 servings.

# Strawberry Ambrosia

Ambrosia in the name of a fruit salad indicates the presence of cocoanut. Fresh cocoanut is easy to grate in a food processor.

2 large seedless oranges
2 cups (500 mL) hulled
  strawberries
2 Tbs (25 mL) granulated sugar

¼ cup (60 mL) shredded cocoanut, fresh if possible
2 Tbs (25 mL) orange liqueur,
  brandy or rum

Grate off ½ tsp (3 mL) of the orange rind. Reserve. Peel the oranges, cut off the papery outer membrane and slice thinly. There should be 1½ cups (375 mL) of slices.

Layer the oranges and berries in a glass bowl, sprinkling each layer with some of the rind, sugar, cocoanut and liquor. Cover and chill 2 hours. Serve with whipped cream, yogurt or sour cream.

Yields 5 to 6 refreshing servings.

# Strawberries with Whipped Cream Strawberry Sauce

4 cups (1 L) hulled strawberries
1 Tbs (15 mL) granulated sugar
2 Tbs (25 mL) brandy
1 cup (250 mL) heavy cream

Purée 1 cup (250 mL) of the smaller berries to make a smooth sauce; stir in the sugar and brandy. Cover and chill. Place the larger berries in an attractive glass bowl; cover and chill until serving time.

Just before serving, whip the cream to soft but firm peaks. Fold in the puréed berries, leaving swirls of the berry sauce in the cream. Gently scrape into a smaller glass bowl. To serve, spoon berries into individual serving dishes and pass the sauce.

Yields 4 to 5 servings.

# Fresh Strawberry Baskets with Sour Cream Sauce

5 cups (1.25 L) unhulled
  strawberries
2 or 3 handfuls fresh mint sprigs

DIPPING SAUCE:
1 cup (250 mL) sour cream
1 tsp (5 mL) grated lemon rind
1 tsp (5 mL) lemon juice
1 cup (250 mL) demerara or light
  brown sugar or grated maple
  sugar

Rinse the berries and set to dry on towelling. Rinse the mint, shake off the moisture, wrap in towelling and chill.

Combine the cream, lemon rind and juice. Place in a pretty bowl; cover and chill.

To serve, line individual baskets with mint leaves, fill with berries and serve accompanied by the sour cream sauce and the sugar. Hold onto each berry by the hull and dip first into the sauce, then into the sugar before you eat it.

Yields 3 to 4 servings.

# Strawberries with Wine Custard Sauce

A sauce that turns a bowl of berries into a party — and it's just as flattering to raspberries, blackberries or blueberries.

8 to 10 cups (2 to 2.5 L) hulled
  strawberries, blueberries,
  blackberries or raspberries
6 egg yolks
¾ cup (175 mL) granulated sugar

¾ cup (175 mL) medium sherry
  or white vermouth
1 cup (250 mL) heavy cream
  or 3 egg whites

Place the strawberries in 8 to 10 individual serving dishes; glass ones are the most attractive. Cover and keep chilled.

Beat the egg yolks and sugar together until light and straw-coloured. Mix in the sherry. Pour into the top of a double boiler and set over simmering water. Cook, whipping constantly with a whisk or beater, until thickened and fluffy, like soft whipped cream. Remove from the heat and continue to whip until completely cold. A fast way to do this is to set the saucepan in a large bowl of ice cubes.

Whip the cream to soft peaks, or the egg whites to stiff but not dry peaks. If using the whipped cream, fold it gently into the wine custard; if using the egg whites, first stir a quarter of them into the custard, then fold the custard into the remaining whites. Use within the hour as a sauce over the berries.

Yields 8 to 10 servings.

# Honeydew Melon and Blueberries with Yogurt, Honey and Ginger Dressing

1 medium-large honeydew melon (cantaloupe is good, too)
1¼ cups (300 mL) blueberries, hulled strawberries, black-berries, raspberries, or a combination of berries
⅓ cup (75 mL) white vermouth

DRESSING:
1¼ cups (300 mL) plain yogurt
1 Tbs (15 mL) liquid clover honey
¼ cup (50 mL) chopped crystallized or chopped drained preserved ginger

Halve and seed the melon. Divide into 6 pieces, peel off the rind and any tough flesh close to it, and cut into baby finger-sized pieces.

Place about a third of the melon in the bottom of a bowl, preferably a glass one, add a third of the berries and sprinkle on a third of the vermouth. Make two more layers; cover and chill 2 hours.

Combine the ingredients for the dressing. Cover and chill for 2 hours. To serve, spoon out the melon and berries into individual bowls and top with some of the dressing.

Yields 6 servings.

# Blueberry Sauce

An easy sauce to make with fresh or unsweetened frozen berries. And it has many uses — over ice cream, yogurt, cake and Crêpes (page 55); as a sauce with the Victorian Vanilla Cream (page 62); or as a sauce instead of the blackberry glaze for Imperial Blackberry Cheesecake (page 37).

3 cups (750 mL) blueberries
2 tsp (10 mL) cornstarch
½ cup (125 mL) granulated sugar
1 tsp (5 mL) grated lemon rind
½ tsp (3 mL) grated orange rind

1 Tbs (15 mL) lemon juice
pinch of salt
⅛ tsp (0.5 mL) freshly grated nutmeg
1 Tbs (15 mL) butter

Pour the blueberries into a heavy-bottomed saucepan. Blend the cornstarch into the sugar and stir into the berries. Add the remaining ingredients and place over medium heat. Cook, stirring frequently, until the berries are tender and sauce slightly thickened. Cool. If not used immediately, store in an airtight container in the refrigerator.

Yields about 3 cups (750 mL).

# Sherried Cranberry Sauce

⅓ cup (75 mL) slivered orange peel, outer zest only
2 cups (500 mL) boiling water
1½ cups (375 mL) granulated sugar

⅔ cup (150 mL) cold water
⅓ cup (75 mL) sherry or port
1 Tbs (15 mL) lemon juice
3 cups (750 mL) cranberries

Combine the zest and boiling water in a saucepan. Cook for 3 minutes over high heat, remove from the heat and drain. Discard the liquid.

Blend the sugar, cold water, sherry and lemon juice in a large saucepan. Bring to the boil over high heat, reduce the heat and simmer 5 minutes. Add the cranberries and the blanched zest and cook, bubbling briskly over moderately high heat, until the cranberries have popped. This usually takes about 5 minutes. Cool and store in an airtight container in the refrigerator.

Yields about 4 cups (1 L).

# Whole Berry Cranberry Sauce

Here is an unusual way to prepare cranberry sauce so that the berries stay plump and whole. The vital secret: don't uncover or jiggle the sauce until it's thoroughly cooled. A good idea is to make it in the evening and leave it in the saucepan on the cold stove until morning.

1 cup (250 mL) water
1½ cups (375 mL) granulated
  sugar

½ tsp (3 mL) grated lemon or
  orange rind
4 cups (1 L) cranberries

Combine the first 3 ingredients in a heavy-bottomed saucepan. Stir and bring to a gentle boil. When the sugar has dissolved, add the cranberries, stir gently and bring back to the boil slowly, over medium heat.

Cover tightly, reduce heat to low, and cook at a bare simmer for 15 minutes. Remove from the heat and let cool 12 hours before removing the cover.

Spoon into serving dishes or, for storage in the refrigerator, into an airtight container.

Yields about 5 cups (1.25 L).

# Fresh Cranberry Fruit Relish

This is the classic accompaniment to turkey for those who like a tangy sauce.

½ orange
1 large unpeeled apple,
  Northern Spy recommended

2 cups (500 mL) cranberries
1 cup (250 mL) granulated sugar

Divide the orange half into 4 pieces. Remove the seeds. Quarter the apple; remove the stem, blossom end and core. Grind the orange, apple and cranberries in a food grinder, or chop in a food processor, using the steel blade. Transfer the fruit into a large bowl and stir in the sugar. Leave at room temperature for an hour, stirring frequently to dissolve the sugar.

Scrape into an airtight container and store in the refrigerator at least 2 hours before serving. This relish keeps well in the refrigerator for 2 weeks.

Yields 2½ cups (625 mL).

# Classic Cranberry Sauce

There's no reason to restrict cranberry sauce to the fowl season, October to December. Because of the cranberry's natural pectin and acid, it makes a lovely thick sauce that keeps well, sealed like jam in sterilized jars. Use it for topping cheesecakes, heat and thin it with some white wine and fill crêpes, add some to poultry stuffing, or glaze duck, ham slices, pork chops or roasts.

4 cups (1 L) cranberries
1 cup (250 mL) water
2 cups (500 mL) granulated sugar

Place the cranberries and water in a large high-sided saucepan. Set over high heat and bring to the boil, then reduce the heat and boil gently until the cranberries are tender, about 5 to 8 minutes.

Add the sugar and stir well; increase the heat and bring back to the boil. Cook until the sauce is thick and dark red, about 8 minutes.

For use within 2 weeks, cool and pour into containers, cover and refrigerate. For longer storage, pour into hot sterilized jars and seal; see Method I on page 88. Alternate techniques are acceptable.

Yields three 8 oz (250 mL) jars.


# Fresh Raspberry Sauce

3 cups (750 mL) raspberries
2 Tbs (25 mL) Red Currant Jelly
  (page 105)
¼ cup (50 mL) icing sugar

2 Tbs (25 mL) brandy or raspberry
  brandy (framboise) or orange
  liqueur

There are two ways of tackling this incredibly easy but delicious sauce. The first is simply to place all the ingredients in a food processor or blender and whirl together until smooth. Cover and chill.

But for the ultimate sauce, strain out the seeds. The best way to do this is to purée the berries and jelly in the blender or food processor, then press through a sieve. Then combine the seedless purée with the sugar and liqueur.

To make the sauce without a blender or food processor, press the whole berries, a few handfuls at a time, and the jelly through a sieve, or pass through the fine disk of a food mill. Combine with the sugar and liqueur.

The sauce may be prepared up to 8 hours in advance; stir before serving.

Serve with good vanilla ice cream and peach halves, fresh or poached pears, or whole strawberries. Other uses abound: serve whipped cream instead of ice cream with the fruit, or scoop ice cream into meringue shells and top with sauce.

Yields about 2 cups (500 mL) sauce.

## Blackberry Sauce

Substitute blackberries for the raspberries in Fresh Raspberry Sauce. Sieve out the seeds.

## Fresh Strawberry Sauce

4 cups (1 L) hulled strawberries
½ cup (125 mL) granulated sugar
3 Tbs (45 mL) brandy or kirsch

Slice half the berries into a bowl. Purée the remaining berries, add to the sliced ones and mix in the sugar and brandy. Let stand at room temperature for 30 minutes, stirring periodically to dissolve the sugar. Cover and chill until serving time.

Yields about 3½ cups (875 mL).

# How to Make Sherbets and Water Ices

Prepare the fruit according to the directions in each recipe and make sure that all ingredients are cool before proceeding with the freezing.

Scrape the fruit mixture into shallow pans (cake pans or freezer trays are good) to a depth of about 1" (2.5 cm). Set level in a freezer, and freeze until there is a solid frozen border around the edge of the pan but the centre is still mushy. This stage usually takes about 1 to 1½ hours but the time can vary depending on the freezer temperature and the location of the pans in the freezer.

The next step is the important one of breaking down the ice crystals. Break up the hard frozen part and spoon about half, along with about half of the mushy centre, into a blender, the work bowl of a food processor, or a large mixing bowl. Chilling the bowl or blender jar is a good idea. Twirl or beat until the mixture is completely broken down, smooth and creamy-looking. With a blender or food processor, it may be necessary to stop the machine and scrape the still frozen pieces down closer to the blades. It is important to work quickly so that the sherbet does not melt.

Pack the smooth mixture into a container for freezing; cover. Deal with the second half of the sherbet the same way. Store in the freezer.

Homemade fruit sherbets taste best when freshly made and are easier to serve and eat when not too hard. Eat the sherbet within 2 to 3 hours after it has been repacked into the freezer containers, or allow to soften 20 minutes in the refrigerator before serving.

# Ripe Gooseberry Water Ice

2½ cups (625 mL) gooseberries
1 cup (250 mL) granulated sugar
1 cup (250 mL) water

2 Tbs (30 mL) lemon juice
⅛ tsp (0.5 mL) salt

Combine the gooseberries, sugar and water in a saucepan. Cover and bring to the boil. Reduce heat immediately and simmer gently 5 minutes, or until the berries are tender. Press through a coarse sieve or the medium disk of a food mill.

Cool the purée and combine with remaining ingredients. Turn into a cake pan or freezer trays and proceed according to the instructions above. Yields 4 to 5 servings.

# Strawberry Water Ice

1 cup (250 mL) granulated sugar
2 cups (500 mL) water
3½ cups (875 mL) hulled
  strawberries

2 Tbs (25 mL) lemon juice
½ tsp (3 mL) orange flower water
  (optional)

Combine the sugar and water in a saucepan and bring to the boil over high heat. Reduce heat to medium and boil gently for 5 minutes. Remove from the heat and cool.

Purée the berries in a medium sieve, food processor, blender, or food mill, using a fine disk. (If a seedless water ice is desired, use a sieve or a food mill, or purée mechanically and press the purée through a fine sieve.) There should be at least 2 cups (500 mL) purée.

Incorporate the sugar syrup into the purée, and add the lemon juice and orange flower water. Pour into cake pans and proceed according to the instructions on page 78.

Yields 6 servings.


# Red Currant Ice

4 cups (1 L) stemmed red currants
1½ cups (375 mL) water
1¼ cups (300 mL) granulated
  sugar

2 Tbs (25 mL) lemon juice
¼ cup (50 mL) orange juice

Combine the red currants and water in a saucepan. Cover and bring to the boil over high heat, then reduce the heat and simmer for 10 minutes. Using a medium sieve, strain out all the skins and seeds, pressing to extract all the juice. There should be at least 2 cups (500 mL) of juice.

Wash out the saucepan and return the currant juice to it. Stir in the sugar. Heat at medium temperature just long enough to dissolve the sugar. Add the citrus juices; cool.

Pour into cake pans and proceed according to the instructions on page 78.

Yields 6 servings.

# Black Currant Ice

1½ cups (375 mL) black currants
2 cups (500 mL) water
1 cup (250 mL) granulated sugar

1 Tbs (15 mL) lemon juice
⅛ tsp (0.5 mL) salt
3 egg whites

Place the currants and 1 cup (250 mL) of the water in a saucepan. Cover and bring to the boil. Reduce the heat to low and simmer 15 minutes, or until mushy. Press through a medium sieve or the fine disk of a food mill. Discard the seeds and skins; cool.

Meanwhile, combine the remaining water with the sugar. Bring to the boil and continue boiling 5 minutes. Cool and combine with the black currant purée, lemon juice and salt. Proceed according to the instructions on page 78. The semi-frozen purée has a gorgeous creamy reddish-purple colour.

Beat the egg whites until stiff but not dry, and fold gently but thoroughly into the sherbet at the semi-frozen purée stage. Pack into containers and freeze.

Yields 8 servings.

# Raspberry Water Ice

¾ cup (175 mL) granulated sugar
¾ cup (175 mL) water
2½ cups (625 mL) raspberries

2 Tbs (30 mL) lemon juice
⅛ tsp (0.5 mL) salt
2 egg whites

Combine the sugar and water in a saucepan. Bring to the boil and boil for 5 minutes. Cool. Purée the berries; mix with the lemon juice and salt. Pour into a shallow cake pan or freezer trays.

Proceed according to the instructions on page 78. Beat the egg whites to stiff but not dry peaks; fold in at the semi-frozen purée stage.

Yields 6 to 8 servings.

# Tangerine and Cranberry Sherbet

The tartness of the tangerine and cranberries makes this sherbet especially enjoyable. Served scoop for scoop with good vanilla ice cream, it's a satisfying dessert for a late fall brunch.

| 2 tangerines | ½ cup (125 mL) tangerine juice |
| 2 cups (500 mL) cranberries | 1 Tbs (15 mL) orange liqueur |
| 1 cup (250 mL) granulated sugar | (optional, but recommended) |

Remove the seeds and blossom ends from the tangerines and either grind, using the medium blade, or chop in a food processor fitted with the steel blade. Grind or chop the cranberries.

Combine the fruit, sugar and juice and let stand at room temperature, stirring periodically, until the sugar has dissolved. Add the orange liqueur and scrape into a large cake tin. Proceed according to instructions on page 78.

Yields 6 to 8 servings.

# How to Make Ice Cream with a Churn Freezer

Combine the ingredients in the can of a churn freezer. Insert the paddle and put on the lid. Position the can in the churn freezer and clamp on the crank.

Surround the can with layers of crushed ice and coarse salt. Street salt works well and is cheap; coarse pickling salt is next best. Some electric churn freezers call for the finer and more expensive table salt; unless specified, you can use the coarse anyway. Recommended proportions are roughly 4 parts crushed ice to 1 part salt. These ice-salt layers should come to within 1″ (2.5 cm) of the top of the can. Have more crushed ice and salt ready because the ice settles when the churning begins.

Turn the crank slowly at first, and then when the turning becomes more difficult, turn more quickly. Helpers are a must at this stage. Always turn steadily, and maintain the level of ice and salt throughout.

When it becomes almost impossible to turn the crank, after about 15 to 20 minutes, unclamp the crank and remove the can, being careful not to let any of the salty ice into the ice cream. Wipe the can off and remove the lid and paddle. (The person who cranked the most has first dibs at licking the paddle.)

Scoop out the ice cream for immediate gratification or pack it down in the can and store in the freezer. Try to eat it all within 3 to 4 days, as natural ice cream contains no preservative and can become grainy.

# Raspberry Honey Ice Cream

2½ cups (625 mL) raspberries
¾ cup (175 mL) liquid clover
  honey
2 cups (500 mL) milk
¼ tsp (1 mL) salt

4 eggs, well beaten
1 cup (250 mL) light cream
1 cup (250 mL) heavy cream
½ tsp (3 mL) almond extract

Purée the raspberries with a fork, in a food processor fitted with the steel blade, or in a blender. For a less seedy ice cream, press the fruit through a sieve once puréed. Combine with ½ cup (125 mL) of the honey and let stand, covered, 1 to 2 hours at room temperature.

    Combine the milk, the remaining honey and the salt in the top of a double boiler. Bring to the scalding point over direct medium heat. Pour about a quarter of the hot milk onto the eggs, whisking while pouring, then return the milk and eggs to the rest of the milk. Keep beating while pouring. Place over gently simmering water and cook 4 to 8 minutes, stirring constantly, until the custard coats a spoon lightly, at 165°F (74°C). Chill.

    Combine the raspberry purée, custard and remaining ingredients in the can of a churn freezer. Churn according to the directions on page 81.

Yields about 6 to 8 servings.

# Strawberry Ice Cream

1½ cups (375 mL) hulled
  puréed strawberries
1 cup (250 mL) granulated sugar

1 cup (250 mL) heavy cream
1½ cups (375 mL) light cream

Stir the strawberries and sugar together. Cover lightly and let stand 1 to 2 hours at room temperature to mature the flavour.

    Pour the berries and cream into the can of a churn freezer. Churn according to the instructions on page 81.

Yields about 6 servings.

# Saskatoon Soft-Bottom Pudding

This recipe, from Remy Larcombe of Winnipeg, is an example of improvisation using local berries. For a more intense orange flavour, add 2 tsp (10 mL) orange liqueur or 1 tsp (5 mL) grated orange rind.

Almond flavour goes well with saskatoons; you could substitute 3 Tbs (50 mL) water and ½ tsp (3 mL) almond extract for the orange juice. Scatter ¼ cup (50 mL) blanched chopped almonds over the berries for this version.

FRUIT BOTTOM:
3 cups (750 mL) saskatoons
⅓ cup (100 mL) granulated sugar
1 Tbs (15 mL) all-purpose flour
3 Tbs (50 mL) orange juice

BATTER:
½ cup (125 mL) butter
½ cup (125 mL) granulated sugar
1 egg
½ tsp (3 mL) vanilla
1 cup (250 mL) sifted all-
    purpose flour
1 tsp (5 mL) baking powder
¼ tsp (1 mL) salt
½ cup (125 mL) milk

Grease an 8″ x 8″ (2 L) cake pan. Preheat oven to 375°F (190°C).

To prepare the fruit bottom, put the berries in the pan. Combine the sugar and flour and sprinkle over the berries. Drizzle on the orange juice. Set aside.

To make the batter, cream the butter and sugar. Beat in the egg and vanilla. The mixture should be light and fluffy. Sift together the dry ingredients and stir into the batter in 3 portions, alternately with the milk, in 2 portions. Spread evenly over the berries. Bake for 35 minutes, or until the cake is golden and is done when tested with a skewer. Cool slightly before serving, with a pitcher of cream.

Yields 6 to 8 servings.

# Double-Crunch Rhubarb Crisp

This is *the* deluxe version of rhubarb crisp.

CRUMBLE:
1 cup (250 mL) unsifted all-
   purpose flour
1 cup (250 mL) rolled oats
¾ cup (200 mL) firmly packed
   brown sugar
½ cup (125 mL) melted butter
½ tsp (2 mL) cinnamon
½ tsp (2 mL) freshly grated nutmeg
¼ tsp (1 mL) salt

SAUCE:
1 cup (250 mL) granulated sugar
2 Tbs (25 mL) cornstarch
1 cup (250 mL) cold water
1 tsp (5 mL) vanilla

FILLING:
4½ cups (1.125 L) diced rhubarb,
   in ½" (12 mm) pieces

Lightly butter a 9" x 9" (2.5 L) cake tin. Preheat oven to 350°F (180°C).

To prepare the crumble, combine the ingredients in a large bowl. Mix thoroughly. Press half the crumbs over the bottom and sides of the cake tin. Reserve the remaining crumbs.

To make the sauce, blend the sugar and cornstarch together in a small saucepan. Stir in the water, mixing well to eliminate lumps. Bring to the boil, reduce heat, and cook until thick, smooth and clear, about 5 minutes. Whisk constantly. Remove from the heat; add the vanilla.

Place the rhubarb over the bottom layer of crumble, spoon the sauce evenly over the rhubarb and top with remaining crumbs.

Bake for 1 hour, or until the top is a golden crusty brown, the filling bubbles up along the sides and the rhubarb is tender.

Serve warm or hot with a bowl of unsweetened whipped cream, a jug of light cream or vanilla ice cream.

Yields 8 to 10 servings.

# Blueberry Oatmeal Nut Crisp

FRUIT LAYER:
4 cups (1 L) blueberries
¾ cup (175 mL) granulated sugar
1 Tbs (15 mL) lemon juice
1 tsp (5 mL) quick-cooking
  tapioca (optional)

TOPPING:
⅓ cup (75 mL) all-purpose flour
⅓ cup (75 mL) firmly packed
  brown sugar
¾ cup (175 mL) rolled oats
¼ cup (50 mL) unblanched
  chopped almonds
1 tsp (5 mL) cinnamon
⅓ cup (75 mL) cold butter

Preheat oven to 350°F (180°C). Combine the ingredients for the fruit layer in a 9" x 9" (2.5 L) cake pan.

Mix all the dry ingredients for the topping together in a large bowl. Cut in the butter, working until the mixture forms large crumbs. Spread evenly over the top of the fruit.

Bake for 40 to 45 minutes, or until the berry filling is bubbling up and the top is crisp and golden.

Serve warm or cold with a pitcher of cream or scoops of good vanilla ice cream.

Yields 6 servings.

# Cranberry Duff

This pudding just might start the renaissance of steamed puddings in Canada. Just enough spice, molasses, cranberries, raisins and nuts in a light batter — unlike the heavy, doughy concoctions that give steamed puddings a bad name.

1⅔ cups (400 mL) sifted all-purpose flour
1 tsp (5 mL) baking powder
½ tsp (3 mL) salt
1¼ cups (300 mL) halved cranberries
1 cup (250 mL) raisins (seeded ones are best)

½ cup (125 mL) chopped fresh walnuts
½ cup (125 mL) cold butter
½ cup (125 mL) molasses
2 tsp (10 mL) baking soda
½ cup (125 mL) boiling water
1 recipe Whiskey Pudding Sauce (below)

Butter a 5 cup (1.25 L) pudding bowl or mould.

Sift the first 3 ingredients into a large bowl. Combine the cranberries, raisins and nuts in another bowl. Sprinkle 2 Tbs (25 mL) of the dry ingredients over the fruit and nuts and toss well to coat all the pieces. Set this bowl aside for the moment.

Cut the butter into the sifted dry ingredients, working until the mixture is crumbly.

Measure the molasses in a large measuring cup, add the soda and the boiling water and stir as the mixture foams up. Pour all at once over the dry ingredients. Dump in the fruit and nuts and mix together just enough to blend.

Turn into the prepared bowl. Cover the surface of the dough with a round of lightly buttered wax paper. Cover the bowl with aluminum foil, with a 1" (2.5 cm) pleat along the middle. (The pleat allows for expansion as the pudding rises.) Tie firmly around the edge of the bowl with string.

Place on a rack in a large saucepan. Pour enough boiling water into the saucepan to come two-thirds of the way up the bowl. Cover, bring to the boil and adjust the heat so that the water boils moderately vigorously. Steam for 2 hours. Add more boiling water if necessary in order to maintain the level.

Serve hot with Whiskey Pudding Sauce.

Yields 6 servings for winter appetites.

# Whiskey Pudding Sauce

½ cup (125 mL) butter
1 cup (250 mL) icing sugar
4 Tbs (60 mL) light cream

1 Tbs (15 mL) whiskey
1 tsp (5 mL) vanilla

Beat the butter until light and creamy, gradually beating in the sugar. When the mixture is very light and fluffy begin adding the cream, 1 Tbs (15 mL) at a time. Finally beat in the whiskey and vanilla.

Place the bowl containing the sauce in a large bowl of medium-hot water and beat just long enough to soften and become smooth. Serve at once.

Yields enough for 1 pudding.

# Cranberry Apples

An easy fall dessert that can bake in the oven along with a main course and vegetables.

6 medium-large apples, Northern
  Spy recommended
2 Tbs (30 mL) butter

2 cups (500 mL) Classic Cranberry
  Sauce (page 76)
½ cup (125 mL) water

Preheat oven to 350°F (180°C).

Core the apples; pare a third of the way down, to prevent the apples from bursting. Place in a shallow heatproof dish just big enough to accommodate them comfortably.

Distribute the butter evenly into the cores of the apples. Combine the sauce and water; spoon over and around the apples.

Bake for 45 to 60 minutes, basting frequently. Baked apples are at their best while still warm from the oven, with a pitcher of cream.

Yields 6 servings.

# PRESERVING

## Preserving Jams and Jellies

Most preserves can be safely stored in a dark, cool and dry place for about a year if these steps are followed.

First, select the jars, always allowing two or three extra, to be on the safe side. Wash the jars, lids, funnel and ladle in warm, soapy water, then rinse in clear water. Dry the lids and reserve. Then place everything else in a large saucepan, cover with boiling water and boil 15 minutes. If the jars aren't needed right away, reduce the heat to minimum and keep the jars under the very hot water until ready to be filled. Remove the jars with tongs and drain and set upright.

An easier method of sterilizing the jars is to place them upright on a tray and set in an oven at 225°F (110°C) for 15 minutes. Turn the heat off, leaving the jars in the hot oven until ready to be filled.

There are at least three possible methods of sealing your preserves once the jars are sterilized. I have indicated the best sealing method for each recipe in this section.

### METHOD I
Fill the jars to within ½" (12 mm) of the top, using the ladle and funnel and making absolutely sure that none of the jam dribbles on the inside of the jar above that level. Pour a thin layer of melted wax over the surface and tilt and rotate the jar so that the wax adheres to the glass and makes a seal. Cool to harden, then pour on a second thin layer of wax, again tilting and rotating the jar. Put on the lid and store in a dark, cool and dry place.

I have found this method of "bottling" jam and jelly to be straight-forward and safe under good storage conditions.

### METHOD II
A second method of filling and sealing requires "canning" jars. Use one of the above methods of sterilization for the jars, but in addition drop clean, new canning jar lids into boiling water and leave them there, off the heat, to allow the circle of sealing compound to soften. When filling each jar with the jam, jelly or relish, leave a ⅛" (3 mm) headspace. Immediately screw the lid on tightly, then flip the jar over and back

again. Set to cool on a rack. When the jam has cooled, check the seal to make sure the lid on the jar has concaved. If it has not, refrigerate the contents and use within a month.

METHOD III
The safest method for sealing jars, useful when storage conditions are not ideal, is good for jams, relishes, some pickles and particularly preserved fruit. Use canning jars with new lids.

Boil the jam to just below the setting point (220°F, 104°C on a jam or candy thermometer), then pour into hot, clean jars, leaving a ¼" (6 mm) headspace. Wipe the edge of the jar with a clean damp cloth. Set the jar lids, previously softened in boiling water as described for Method II, on the jars and tighten. Set on a rack in a canner, sometimes called a boiling water bath. Fill with water to a level 1" (2.5 cm) above the top of the jars. Cover the canner, bring to the boil over high heat and boil hard for 15 minutes. Remove the jars, cool on a rack and check the seals.

JELLY BAGS
The recipes for jellies, syrups and juices call for a dampened jelly bag. One can be made easily out of a square yard (metre) of factory cotton; fold and sew it into a triangular shape that looks like an upside-down witch's cap. You can also substitute a double layer of dampened cheesecloth, suspended in a large sieve or colander. Let the juices drip out for 3 to 4 hours or overnight, if more convenient.

HOW TO TELL WHEN IT'S DONE
For jelly, this is easy — use a candy thermometer. Boil the mixture to 220°F (104°C), the setting point, and proceed to fill the jelly jars, following Method I or Method II.

There is also a classic test for jelly. Stir the boiling jelly, then hold the stirring spoon up horizontally, well above the heat of the jelly. At first the boiling syrup will flow off the spoon in two distinct streams. Keep stirring and testing. Gradually the two streams will slow down and merge. The jelly reaches the gelling point, or is said to "sheet," when two drips of the jelly come together in the middle in a wide heavy drop and hang suspended, but quite firm, from the spoon.

For jams the setting point is reached at the same temperature as jellies, i.e., at 220°F (104°C). A handy test that can be done without a thermometer is the "wrinkle" test. Before starting to boil the jam, place a medium-sized plate in the freezer. Then, as the jam thickens, begin testing. Remove the plate from the freezer and the jam from the heat. Spoon a thin dab of jam, about the size of a nickel, onto the plate. Cool briefly. Run a finger through the jam, and if wrinkles form in the jam along the side where it has been pushed, the jam is set. If the jam does not wrinkle, continue the boiling and return the plate to the freezer. Retest again until a satisfactory set has been reached. Always put the dab of jam on a clean part of the plate.

## Freezing Berries

It's tempting to freeze a lot of berries; they taste and look so great in the summer. It seems an even better idea when the garden or a trip to a pick-your-own farm or the wilds provides a sudden glut of free or bargain-priced fruit. However, the freezing process cannot improve the flavour and texture of fresh berries, so unless the fruit is really abundant, in excellent condition, cheap or unobtainable except by home freezing, it is often more economical to buy small amounts of commercially frozen fruit when you need it in the off-season. But aside from economic considerations, the advantage in home freezing is that you are able to control the quantity of sugar used. Many of the soft summer fruits freeze well without any sugar at all. They are the ultimate versatile ingredient, easy to pop into cakes, pies, sauces, puddings, ice cream, savoury dishes and even preserves; and you won't have to calculate how much sweetener must be deducted from the recipe. In addition, there's no discounting the usefulness of having a supply of frozen fruit for emergency meals or extra touches.

The technique described on page 108 for freezing strawberries is also successful for raspberries, chopped rhubarb, blueberries, blackberries, gooseberries, partridgeberries and saskatoons. This method of freezing the berries separately before packing them into bags ensures that fruit will not clump together and will flow out of the bags. This reduces thawing time. Red and black currants can also be frozen this way, but often it is just as easy to pack them into conveniently sized bags and freeze. Cranberries should simply be bagged (you could keep them in the bags they came in) and frozen straight away. Thaw at room temperature or in the refrigerator.

Some people do like their frozen berries sweetened, so here are ratios of granulated sugar and berries suited to this method.

Combine berries and sugar in a large bowl in the following propor-tions; 4 cups (1 L) raspberries and ½ cup (125 mL) sugar, 4 cups (1 L) blueberries or sliced strawberries and ⅔ cup (150 mL) sugar, or 4 cups (1 L) gooseberries or chopped rhubarb and 1 cup (250 mL) sugar. Pack the fruit into 2 cup (500 mL) bags, suck out the air with a straw and tie.

To thaw, set in the refrigerator for 6 to 8 hours or 1 hour in a dish under cold water. It is best to eat frozen fruit before it is completely thawed and while it still has some ice crystals; but for pies, baked puddings, stewed fruit and sauces, thaw just long enough to separate the pieces and proceed as for fresh fruit.

## Blueberry Red Currant Jam

I like to combine blueberries with other fruit when making jam. Red currants are a good companion, not only because of the zip they add to the taste, but also because they provide the gelling power blueberries lack.

| | |
|---|---|
| 4 cups (1 L) blueberries | 2 cups (500 mL) water |
| 2 cups (500 mL) stemmed red currants | 3 cups (750 mL) granulated sugar |

Place the blueberries in a large saucepan and the red currants in a medium saucepan. Pour 1 cup (250 mL) of water into each saucepan. Cover the currants. Bring each to the boil, then reduce the heat so that the fruit in each pan simmers gently. Remove the blueberries from the heat after 5 minutes; reserve. Simmer the currants 10 minutes, remove from the heat and press through a medium sieve or the fine disk of a food mill to remove the seeds. Add the currant purée to the blueberries.

Bring the mixture slowly to a gentle boil, over medium heat; simmer for 5 minutes. Stir in the sugar, increase the heat to high and boil vigorously until the jam thickens and sets, about 10 minutes (see page 89). Stir frequently all through the cooking period.

Pour into hot sterilized jars and seal using Method I on page 88. The other methods are acceptable.

Yields about five 8 oz (250 mL) jars.

# Blackberry Jelly

Proceed as for Raspberry Jelly (page 100), using fresh blackberry juice. Start with 12 cups (3 L) whole blackberries, crushed, to get 4 cups (1 L) blackberry juice. Omit the lemon juice.

# Blueberry Tangerine Marmalade

The tangerine and lemon skins must be softened in water before they can be combined with the blueberries and sugar. In the winter, which is when tangerines are more easily available, you can make this marmalade with unsweetened frozen blueberries. Thaw them and proceed; no need to crush.

| | |
|---|---|
| 3 large tangerines or 2 oranges | 4 cups (1 L) blueberries |
| 1 lemon | 1 box pectin crystals |
| ⅛ tsp (0.5 mL) baking soda | 6 cups (1.5 L) granulated sugar |
| 1¼ cups (300 mL) water | |

Squeeze out the tangerine and lemon juice. Remove the seeds and reserve the juice. There should be 1¼ cups (300 mL).

Chop the peel with a knife or in a food processor, using a steel blade; or cut with scissors into very thin slivers. There should be 1¼ cups (300 mL) peel. If the quantity of either juice or peel is short, use more tangerines or oranges.

Place the slivered peel, baking soda and water in a preserving kettle. Cover, bring to a steaming simmer over medium heat, then adjust the heat so that the mixture just barely simmers for 45 minutes. The peel should be translucent and tender. Add the reserved juice.

Crush the berries thoroughly, and add to the citrus fruit. Thoroughly blend in the pectin crystals. Place over high heat and bring to the simmering point. Adjust the heat so that the mixture simmers 1 minute. Stir often.

Increase the heat to maximum, bringing to a vigorous tumbling boil, and immediately stir in all the sugar. Bring back to a rolling boil and cook exactly 1 minute.

Remove from the heat, skim with a large metal spoon and stir for 7 minutes to distribute the fruit throughout the marmalade. Continue to skim during the stirring period.

Pour into hot sterilized jars and seal; see Method I on page 88. Method II is acceptable.

Yields about eight 8 oz (250 mL) jars.

## Cranberry Rum Conserve

A favourite recipe among the students in my Jams, Jellies and Pickles class.

1 orange
2 cups (500 mL) water
3 cups (750 mL) granulated sugar
4 cups (1 L) cranberries
½ cup (125 mL) raisins

½ cup (125 mL) blanched
  chopped almonds (optional)
¼ cup (50 mL) rum or orange
  liqueur

Quarter the orange and remove seeds and blossom end. Chop finely in a grinder or food processor, using the steel blade. Combine with the water in a medium saucepan and bring to the boil over high heat. Adjust the heat to let the orange simmer uncovered, for 20 minutes. The peel should be tender and the water somewhat reduced.

Scrape into a large heavy-bottomed saucepan, add the sugar, cranberries and raisins and bring slowly to the boil over medium heat. Increase the heat and boil rapidly until thick and gelled, about 6 to 8 minutes. Add the nuts, if desired, 2 minutes after the mixture comes to the boil. Stir constantly. Remove from the heat, stir in the rum and ladle into hot sterilized jars. Seal using Method I on page 88; the other methods are acceptable.

Yields about eight 4 oz (125 mL) jars.

# Cranberry Mincemeat

A dark, garnet-red mincemeat that's tart and lemony, not too spicy. Recommended in this Thirties recipe as having "exceptionally good keeping qualities." Frankly, it's too good to last.

2 cups (500 mL) cider
1 cup (250 mL) butter
2 cups (500 mL) firmly packed
brown sugar
3 cups (750 mL) cranberries
3 cups (750 mL) peeled cored
chopped apples
1 orange, quartered, seeded and
ground
3 cups (750 mL) raisins (seeded
are the tastiest)
4 cups (1 L) currants
1 cup (250 mL) chopped candied
citron peel

1 cup (250 mL) chopped candied
orange peel
½ cup (125 mL) chopped candied
lemon peel
1 cup (250 mL) halved candied
cherries or sliced candied
pineapple
1 tsp (5 mL) cinnamon
1 tsp (5 mL) freshly grated
nutmeg
½ cup (125 mL) sherry or brandy

Pour the cider into a large heavy-bottomed saucepan. Boil 5 minutes. Add all the remaining ingredients except the sherry. Cover and return slowly to the boil over medium heat. Stir frequently. Uncover and reduce the heat so that the mincemeat simmers very gently for 30 minutes. By this time the cranberries should all have popped and the mincemeat will have thickened and become glossy.

Remove from the heat and stir in the sherry. Cool and store in airtight glass or plastic containers for up to 2 months in the refrigerator.

For longer storage at room temperature, pour the hot mincemeat into clean hot canning jars, leaving a ¼" (6 mm) headspace. Process in a canner, boiling for 25 minutes; see Method III, page 89.

This can be used to make Cranberry Mincemeat Pie (page 20).

Yields 11 cups (2.75 L) mincemeat.

# Black Currant Jelly

For fans of black currants who want the sheer sensation of the flavour.

8 cups (2 L) black currants
8 cups (2 L) water
4 cups (1 L) granulated sugar

Combine the currants and water in a large saucepan. Cover and simmer until the fruit is soft, about 10 to 15 minutes. Crush periodically.

Wet a jelly bag, wring it out and fill it with the black currant pulp. Let the juice drip out 3 to 4 hours. Squeeze the bag if you're determined to extract all the juice, but beware in that case of achieving cloudy jelly.

Measure out 4 cups (1 L) juice and pour into a preserving kettle. Bring to the boil over high heat and boil hard 3 minutes. Stir in the sugar, bring back to the boil and boil vigorously until the jelly sheets; see page 89. This usually takes about 5 minutes with tart black currants.

Remove from the heat, skim with a metal spoon and fill hot sterilized jars. Seal using Method I, page 88; Method II is acceptable.

Yields about six 6 oz (175 mL) jars for every 4 cups (1 L) juice.

# Overnight Black Currant Jam

Black currants will toughen and ruin your jam unless the skins are first tenderized. A preliminary cooking and an overnight soak should solve this problem nicely.

3 cups (750 mL) black currants
2 cups (500 mL) water
5 cups (1.25 L) granulated sugar

Combine the currants and water in a saucepan, place over high heat and bring to the boil. Reduce the heat and simmer, uncovered, for 10 minutes. Cool and pour into a bowl. Cover and let stand overnight.

Pour into a preserving kettle, stir in the sugar and bring to a rapid boil over high heat. Continue boiling for 2 minutes, then skim and remove from the heat. Stir constantly for 5 minutes, then pour into hot sterilized jars. Seal using Method I on page 88; the other methods are acceptable.

Yields five 8 oz (250 mL) jars.

# Gooseberry Chutney

This chutney goes exceptionally well with tourtière. Use red or green gooseberries; either way the chutney will end up a beautiful mahogany brown.

4½ cups (1.125 L) firmly packed
  brown sugar
½ tsp (2 mL) salt
1 cup (250 mL) cider vinegar
½ cup (125 mL) water
2 whole allspice berries
2" (5 cm) piece cinnamon stick,
  broken up

8 whole cloves
¼ tsp (2 mL) freshly grated
  nutmeg
10 cups (2.5 L) topped and
  tailed gooseberries

Combine the sugar, salt, vinegar and water in a preserving kettle. Tie the spices up in a double thickness of rinsed cheesecloth. Hit the bag two or three times with a rolling pin to help release the flavours. Drop into the kettle.

Bring to the boil over high heat, reduce the heat and simmer 5 minutes. Add the berries, bring back to the boil, then adjust the heat so that the chutney bubbles moderately. Stir very frequently. When the syrup has thickened and the berries are tender, after about 40 minutes, remove the spice bag and fill hot sterilized canning jars; see Method II on page 88; Method III is acceptable.

Yields about six 8 oz (250 mL) jars.

# Ripe Gooseberry and Honey Jelly

A clear, deep rosy red jelly with a distinct gooseberry flavour. If a jar can be spared from the breakfast table, use it to glaze fresh fruit tarts. For a jelly with a real bouquet, try adding 1 cup (250 mL) of elderflower heads, packed down, to the gooseberries and water.

12 cups (3 L) gooseberries
1½ cups (375 mL) water
1 box pectin crystals

1 cup (250 mL) liquid clover
  honey
4 cups (1 L) granulated sugar

Combine the gooseberries and water in a large saucepan. Cover and bring to the boil, then reduce the heat immediately and simmer 10 minutes. Stir and crush twice as the berries soften. Wet a jelly bag, wring it out and ladle the fruit into it. Let the juice drip out 3 to 4 hours. Measure; there should be 4½ cups (1.125 L). If there is less juice, it is possible to squeeze the bag to make up the measure, but that could result in cloudy jelly. You could use strained fresh orange juice instead.

Pour the juice into a large preserving kettle; whisk in the pectin crystals. Place over high heat and bring to the boil. Immediately stir in the honey and sugar, then bring back to the boil and boil hard for exactly 1 minute. Remove from the heat and quickly skim off foam with a metal spoon. Pour at once into hot sterilized jars. Seal using Method I on page 88; Method II is acceptable.

Yields eight 8 oz (250 mL) jars.

## Gooseberry and Slivered Orange Marmalade

With young green gooseberries this marmalade gels amazingly fast.

1 orange
¼ cup (50 mL) water
6 cups (1.5 L) green gooseberries
4 cups (1 L) granulated sugar

Cut the zest — that is, the outer rind — off the orange. Sliver finely. Place in a small heavy-bottomed saucepan with the water. Cover and set over low heat for 20 minutes to steep and soften. Add a little more water if necessary to keep the peel from burning.

Meanwhile top and tail the gooseberries. Combine with the sugar in a preserving kettle. Squeeze the juice from the orange; add with the softened peel and any of its liquid. Stir well.

Bring to the boil over high heat and boil vigorously to the gelling point (see page 89). If the gooseberries are really tart, this can happen after about 5 minutes. Fill hot sterilized jars and seal; see Method I on page 88; the other methods are acceptable.

Yields five 8 oz (250 mL) jars.

# Four-Fruit July Jam

This gorgeous jam, often called Jewel Jam because of its ruby colour, is one of Canada's finest traditional preserves. Prepare the fruit leisurely, while sitting out in the garden under a tree.

4 cups (1 L) pitted sour red
cherries
8 cups (2 L) granulated sugar
4 cups (1 L) topped and tailed
green gooseberries

4 cups (1 L) stemmed red
currants
4 cups (1 L) raspberries

Combine the cherries and 2 cups (500 mL) of the sugar in a large preserving kettle. Bring to the boil over high heat and boil vigorously for 5 minutes, stirring almost constantly.

Stir in the gooseberries and another 2 cups (500 mL) of the sugar. Return to the boil and cook 5 minutes. Add the currants, raspberries and the rest of the sugar. Bring back to the boil again, and boil, stirring constantly, until the jam sets, about 5 to 8 minutes (see page 89).

Remove from the heat, skim and stir for 5 minutes. Pour into hot sterilized jars and seal; see Method I on page 88. The other methods are acceptable.

Yields about ten 8 oz (250 mL) jars.

# Classic Raspberry Jam

This jam has a rich red colour, is perfectly firm without being solid and still has the fresh flavour of a hot July raspberry patch. To make Amaretto Raspberry Jam, stir 1 Tbs (15 mL) Amaretto into the jam just before ladling it into the jars.

10 cups (2.5 L) raspberries
8 cups (2 L) granulated sugar
¼ cup (60 mL) lemon juice

Crush the berries in a large preserving kettle and stir in the sugar. Let stand 10 minutes and stir again. Place over high heat. Stirring unflaggingly, bring to a full vigorous boil. Continue boiling and stirring for about 15 minutes, or until the jam has thickened and is a rich red colour (see page 89).

Remove from the heat, mix in the lemon juice and stir for 10 minutes to distribute the seeds throughout the jam. Pour into hot sterilized jars and seal with wax; see Method I on page 88. The other methods are acceptable.

Yields six to seven 8 oz (250 mL) jars.

## Freezer Raspberry Jam

4 cups (1 L) raspberries  
4 cups (1 L) granulated sugar

2 Tbs (30 mL) lemon juice  
½ bottle liquid pectin

Place about a third of the berries in a large bowl. Crush thoroughly with a potato masher or mallet. Add the second and third portions and crush. Measure; there should be 2 cups (500 mL). Crush more if necessary.

Stir the sugar into the berries until well blended. Let stand 15 minutes, then stir again.

Blend the lemon juice and pectin together in a small bowl. Add to the berry mixture and stir continuously for 3 minutes. Ladle immediately into clean jars or freezer containers, leaving a ¼" (6 mm) headspace. Put on tightly fitting lids and let stand to gel for 24 hours at room temperature.

Refrigerate for use within 3 weeks or freeze for longer storage. Allow frozen jam to thaw in the refrigerator before using. Always store open jars of this kind of jam in the refrigerator.

Yields about five 8 oz (250 mL) jars.

## Freezer Strawberry Jam

Proceed as for Freezer Raspberry Jam, but use 1 ¾ cups (450 mL) crushed strawberries instead of the raspberries.

# Rhubarb and Raspberry Jam

This is such an easy jam, with almost no preparation of the fruit, that it's good for the novice jam-maker or for someone in a hurry.

4 cups (1 L) raspberries  
3 cups (750 mL) chopped rhubarb, in ¼" (6 mm) pieces

7 cups (1.75 L) granulated sugar  
½ bottle liquid pectin

Pour the raspberries, 1 cup (250 mL) at a time, into a preserving kettle. Crush each portion thoroughly with a potato masher or mallet. Add the rhubarb and sugar. Mix thoroughly and let stand 3 to 4 hours. Stir.

Place over high heat and bring to a full energetic boil, stirring constantly. Continue to stir and boil hard exactly 1 minute. Remove from the heat and pour in the pectin immediately. Skim and stir for 5 minutes to ensure an even distribution of fruit.

Fill hot sterilized jars and seal; see Method I on page 88. Method II is acceptable.

Yields eight 8 oz (250 mL) jars.


# Raspberry Jelly

12 cups (3 L) raspberries  
¼ cup (50 mL) strained lemon juice

7½ cups (1.875 L) granulated sugar  
1 bottle liquid pectin

Thoroughly crush or purée the berries in a blender or food processor. Wet a jelly bag, wring it out and fill it with the crushed berries. Squeeze out all the juice and measure; there should be 3¾ cups (950 mL).

Pour the raspberry juice, lemon juice and sugar into a preserving kettle. Stir to blend the sugar into the juices. Bring to a full rolling boil over high heat. Stir in the liquid pectin immediately, then bring back to a rolling boil for exactly 1 minute. Remove from the heat and, working quickly, skim off the foam with a cold metal spoon.

Pour quickly into hot sterilized jars and seal; see Method I on page 88. Method II is acceptable.

Yields about eight 8 oz (250 mL) jars.

# Raspberry Black Cherry Conserve

Another stunningly different preserve. The word "conserve" usually indicates the presence of citrus fruit.

3 cups (750 mL) pitted halved
  black cherries
1 orange
water

8 cups (2 L) raspberries
4 cups (1 L) granulated sugar
2 Tbs (25 mL) orange liqueur
  (optional)

Put the cherries in a preserving kettle; cover and place over medium heat. Adjust the heat so that the cherries simmer gently until tender, about 10 minutes. Remove from the heat.

Peel the zest, the thin outer rind, off the orange. Cut enough of it into very fine slivers to make 2 Tbs (30 mL). Place in a small saucepan, cover with water and bring to a boil over high heat. Lower the heat and simmer 3 minutes. Drain thoroughly, discarding the water. Add the orange slivers to the cherries. Use the rest of the orange for another purpose.

Press the raspberries through a medium sieve or the fine disk of a food mill. Measure out 3 cups (750 mL) of this seedless pulp. Add, with the sugar, to the cherries in the preserving kettle; mix well.

Bring to the boil over medium heat, stirring frequently to prevent sticking. Increase the heat to high and boil vigorously with almost constant stirring until the jam thickens, about 15 to 20 minutes (see page 89). Remove from the heat, skim and stir for 5 minutes to disperse the fruit throughout the jam. Add the liqueur.

Ladle into hot sterilized jars; seal using Method I on page 88. The other methods are acceptable.

Yields about five 8 oz (250 mL) jars.

# Raspberry Plum Jam

Anyone with a food processor knows how incredibly useful they are. I find this especially true when preserving; the steel blade is used for chopping fruit like these plums.

4 cups (1 L) finely ground or very finely chopped plums
3 cups (750 mL) raspberries
10 cups (2.5 L) granulated sugar

½ cup (125 mL) lemon or lime juice
1 bottle liquid pectin

Combine the plums, raspberries, sugar and lemon juice in a preserving kettle and stir to blend the sugar into the fruit.

Bring to a full rolling boil over high heat, stirring constantly. Boil exactly 1 minute, then remove from the heat and immediately stir in all the pectin.

Skim and stir for 5 minutes. Ladle into hot sterilized jars and seal using Method I on page 88. Method II is acceptable.

Yields about twelve 8 oz (250 mL) jars.

# Raspberry and Red Currant Jelly

Raspberries alone won't gel but teamed up with red currants they make a superb jelly. Don't waste this jelly on anyone you don't like.

4 cups (1 L) raspberries
8 cups (2 L) stemmed red currants
3½ cups (875 mL) granulated sugar

Place the berries in a large saucepan. Crush thoroughly with a potato masher or mallet. Add half the currants and crush; add the remaining currants and crush again.

Bring to a slow boil over medium heat; simmer gently until the fruit is soft and the juices are running freely, about 10 minutes. Mash again and simmer 2 minutes more.

Wet a jelly bag, wring it out and fill it with the fruit mixture. Let drip 3 to 4 hours. Squeeze to extract 4 cups (1 L) juice.

Combine the juice and sugar in a preserving kettle. Bring to a vigorous boil over high heat. Boil rapidly about 5 minutes, stirring frequently, until the jelly sheets (see page 89).

Pour into hot sterilized jars and seal using Method I on page 88. Method II is acceptable.

Yields four 8 oz (250 mL) jars.

# Red Currant Preserves

Sometimes called "Bar-le-Duc," this red currant jam has some of its seeds and skins removed. The remaining currants are suspended whole in a firm, clear red jelly.

10 cups (2.5 L) stemmed red
  currants
⅓ cup (75 mL) water
7 cups (1.75 L) granulated sugar

Combine 2 cups (500 mL) of the currants with the water in a saucepan. Cook uncovered over moderate heat for about 10 minutes. Mash and stir the currants as they cook until they are soft and translucent.

Wet a jelly bag, wring it out and fill it with the cooked currants. Let the juice drip out, squeezing if necessary to extract 1 cup (250 mL) juice.

Combine this juice with the rest of the red currants and 4 cups (1 L) of the sugar. Mix gently but well and place over high heat. Bring just to the boil, then adjust the heat and simmer for 5 minutes. Remove from the heat and let stand 12 hours in a cool place.

Stir in the remaining sugar and bring slowly to the boil over medium heat. Increase the heat to high and boil, stirring almost constantly, until set, about 30 minutes (see page 89).

Remove from the heat, skim and stir 5 minutes. Pour into hot sterilized jars and seal; see Method I on page 88. The other methods are acceptable.

Yields about nine 8 oz (250 mL) jars.

# Red Currant Marmalade

From Hamiltonian Mary Haslett's nineteenth-century manuscript cookbook — a jelly marmalade that never fails to impress. If I ever had to choose only one red currant preserve to make, this would be it.

8 cups (2 L) stemmed red currants
5 cups (1.25 L) water
2 oranges
4 cups (1 L) granulated sugar

Combine the red currants and 4 cups (1 L) of the water in a large saucepan. Crush thoroughly with a potato masher or mallet. Cover and bring to a boil over high heat, then reduce the heat so that the mixture bubbles gently 10 to 15 minutes. The currants will look bleached and will be deflated.

Wet a jelly bag, wring it out and fill it with the red currant mixture. Let it drip out 3 to 4 hours. Squeeze only if necessary to make 4 cups (1 L) of juice.

Meanwhile pare the zest off the oranges and sliver very finely. There should be about ⅔ cup (150 mL).

Combine the peel and the remaining 1 cup (250 mL) water in a small saucepan. Cover and bring to the boil, then reduce the heat and simmer until the peel is tender and translucent, about 15 to 20 minutes. Drain thoroughly and discard the water.

Combine the currant juice, the tenderized orange peel and the sugar in a preserving kettle, stirring well. Place over high heat, bring to a full rolling boil and continue boiling vigorously until the jelly sheets, about 4 to 10 minutes (see page 89).

Remove from the heat, skim and stir 4 minutes to prevent the peel from rising to the top of the jelly. Pour into hot sterilized jars and seal; see Method I on page 88. Method II is acceptable.

Yields eight 4 oz (125 mL) jars.

# Red Currant Jelly

Proceed as for Red Currant Marmalade, omitting the orange peel. Red currant jelly has many savoury connections. For example, thoroughly blend ½ cup (125 mL) jelly with 3 Tbs (45 mL) prepared horseradish and serve with ham. Or mash ¾ cup (175 mL) jelly with a fork and combine with 1 Tbs (15 mL) chopped fresh mint and 2 tsp (10 mL) grated orange rind to serve with roast lamb.

# Red Currant Conserve

This conserve needs to be processed in a canner. It's best made on the coolest possible July day.

1 orange
½ lemon
¼ cup (50 mL) water

7 cups (1.75 L) stemmed red currants
1½ cups (375 mL) raisins
5 cups (1.25 L) granulated sugar

Quarter the orange and lemon. Remove the seeds and blossom ends. Grind, using a medium blade; or chop medium-fine in a food processor, using the steel blade. Place in a small heavy-bottomed saucepan with the water, cover and steep over very low heat to tenderize the peel. This should take about 20 minutes.

Combine the currants with the citrus fruit, raisins and sugar in a large heavy-bottomed saucepan or preserving kettle. Place over medium heat and cook, stirring frequently, until the sugar has dissolved. Increase the heat to high and boil rapidly to 215°F (102°C), just below the gelling point. Pour immediately into hot sterilized canning jars, leaving a ¼" (6 mm) headspace. Process in a canner, boiling for 15 minutes; see Method III, page 89.

Yields nine 8 oz (250 mL) jars.

# Spiced Rhubarb and Onion Relish

This is surely one of the most published rhubarb recipes since the early 1900s. Its spicy tang and the availability of quantities of rhubarb have made it a favourite of home preservers across the country.

4 cups (1 L) rhubarb, in ¼"
(6 mm) pieces
4 cups (1 L) finely chopped onions
2 cups (500 mL) cider vinegar
4 cups (1 L) firmly packed
brown sugar
1 tsp (5 mL) salt

1 tsp (5 mL) ground allspice
⅛ tsp (0.5 mL) cayenne pepper
½ tsp (3 mL) celery seed
1 tsp (5 mL) cinnamon
¼ tsp (1 mL) ground cloves
½ tsp (3 mL) freshly ground
pepper

Combine the ingredients in a preserving kettle. Stir well. Bring to the boil, stirring frequently, over high heat. Adjust the heat so that the relish bubbles moderately vigorously; stir frequently and remove any scum.

When the relish is a rich brown colour and has the smooth, thick consistency of jam, it is ready. This happens after about 40 to 60 minutes.

Fill hot sterilized canning jars. Flip seal immediately using Method II on page 88. Method III is acceptable.

Yields five 8 oz (250 mL) jars.

# Rhubarb Marmalade

3 oranges
4 cups (1 L) rhubarb, in ¼"
(6 mm) pieces
1 cup (250 mL) seeded raisins

one 19 oz. can (540 g) crushed
pineapple
4½ cups (1.125 L) granulated
sugar

Grate the rind off the oranges, squeeze out the juice and combine the rind and juice with the other ingredients in a large bowl. Mix well, cover and let soak for 12 hours.

Scrape into a large preserving kettle and bring to the boil over high heat, stirring frequently. Boil vigorously until the marmalade has thickened, about 15 minutes.

Fill hot sterilized jars and seal; see Method I on page 88. The other methods are acceptable.

Yields six 8 oz (250 mL) jars.

# Soft Strawberry Jam

It is runny, as its name implies, and has a whole range of uses besides the usual cover for toasts and hot breads. Spread it on crêpes, spoon it over ice cream or use it to sweeten and flavour yogurt.

12 cups (3 L) hulled strawberries
9 cups (2.25 L) granulated sugar

Place the strawberries, 2 cups (500 mL) at a time, in a preserving kettle. Crush each portion with a potato masher or mallet.

Bring slowly to the boil over medium-low heat, stirring frequently. Blend in the sugar and increase the heat to high; bring back to a full rolling boil. Boil for 10 minutes exactly and remove from the heat.

Stir for 5 minutes to disperse the berries throughout the jam. Pour into hot sterilized canning jars, leaving a ¼" (6 mm) headspace. Process in a canner, boiling for 10 minutes; see Method III, page 89.

Yields eight 8 oz (250 mL) jars.

# Overnight Strawberry Jam

Strawberries will rise to the top of the jar if the cooked jam is not stirred until slightly cooled. Stirring while the jam sets suspends the berries evenly throughout the preserve.

4 cups (1 L) hulled sliced berries
6 cups (1.5 L) granulated sugar
½ cup (125 mL) lemon juice

Combine the berries and sugar in a large bowl. Cover and let stand 12 hours. Stir two or three times.

Scrape into a preserving kettle, place over high heat and bring to a boil. Continue boiling vigorously for 5 minutes, stirring continously. Pour in the lemon juice and boil another 3 minutes. Remove from the heat, skim and stir for 5 minutes to distribute the berries throughout the jam.

Fill hot sterilized jars and seal; see Method I on page 88. The other methods are acceptable.

Yields five 8 oz (250 mL) jars.

# Strawberry Cointreau Jam

A little touch of orange liqueur and a pretty jar make this jam a welcome gift. Proceed as for Overnight Strawberry Jam, but add 1 tsp (5 mL) grated orange rind when combining the berries and the sugar. Stir 1 Tbs (15 mL) Cointreau or any other orange liqueur into the jam after it has been skimmed.

# Strawberry and Rhubarb Jam

This combination of fruit is an old Canadian favourite.

4 cups (1 L) hulled strawberries
4 cups (1 L) rhubarb, in ½"
   (12 mm) pieces
6 cups (1.5 L) granulated sugar

Combine the ingredients in a preserving kettle. Let stand 4 hours, stirring occasionally. As the sugar dissolves, juices will flow.

Bring to a rapid boil over high heat, stirring frequently. The jam usually takes about 18 to 20 minutes to thicken and set (see page 89). Remove from the heat; skim and stir 4 minutes.

Pour into hot sterilized jars. Seal using Method I on page 88. The other methods are acceptable.

Yields about five 8 oz (250 mL) jars.

# Freezing Whole Strawberries

Rinse berries briefly in cold water. Hull and place to dry in a single layer on towelling or on fine racks. When they are thoroughly dry, after about an hour, place in single layers on baking sheets and freeze until the berries are firm. Pour into 2 cup (500 mL) freezer bags, suck out the air with a drinking straw or pump, tie very firmly and return to the freezer.

# DRINKS

## Black Currant Spritzer

Summer drinks based on fruit and citric acid enjoyed many years of popularity before the cola and uncola era. Citric acid is inexpensive and easily available in drug stores.

4 cups (1 L) black currants
4 cups (1 L) boiling water
2 Tbs (30 mL) citric acid

2 cups (500 mL) granulated
sugar (approximate)

Chop the black currants in a food processor or grind, blend or crush thoroughly. Place in a glass, enamel or plastic bowl. Pour on the boiling water. Cool and stir in the citric acid. Cover lightly and let stand 24 hours.

Wet a jelly bag and wring it out. Pour the berry pulp into it and let drip through, squeezing to extract all the juice. Measure the juice; combine each cup (250 mL) with ½ cup (125 mL) sugar in a large heavy-bottomed saucepan. Place over high heat, bring to a full rolling boil and boil 3 minutes exactly.

Pour into hot sterilized canning jars, leaving a ¼" (6 mm) headspace. Adjust lids and process in the canner 15 minutes (see page 89). Makes about 4 cups (1 L) syrup.

To serve, combine ¼ cup (60 mL) Spritzer, two or three ice cubes and 8 ounces (250 mL) cold water or soda water in a glass. Stir. Add a lemon slice.

Yields sixteen 8 oz (250 mL) servings.

# Black Currant Juice

Try a squirt of this in a glass of chilled white wine.

4 cups (1 L) black currants
4 cups (1 L) water
1 cup (250 mL) granulated sugar
¼ cup (50 mL) lemon juice

Pour the currants into a large saucepan. Mash, add the water and place over high heat. Cover and bring to the boil; then reduce heat to low and simmer, continuing to mash until the fruit is pulped, 5 to 10 minutes.

Wet a jelly bag and wring it out. Pour the pulp and juice into it and let drip out 3 to 4 hours. Squeeze out any remaining juice.

Combine the currant juice with the sugar and lemon juice in a large saucepan. Bring to the boil over high heat. Pour immediately into hot sterilized canning jars, leaving ¼" (6 mm) headspace. Cover and process 15 minutes in a canner (see page 89). Makes 5 cups (1.25 L) juice.

To serve, dilute 1 part Black Currant Juice in 3 to 4 parts water or soda water. Add a few ice cubes and a slice of lemon.

Yields fifteen to twenty 8 oz (250 mL) servings.

# CranOrange Vodka Punch

The rosiness of this punch makes it a good Christmastime party drink.

2 cups (500 mL) Cranberry Juice
  (page 111)
6 cups (1.5 L) fresh orange juice
¼ cup (60 mL) fresh lime juice

2 cups (500 mL) vodka
2 limes, sliced and seeded
3 trays ice cubes

Combine the fruit juices in a large punch bowl. Cover and chill. At serving time add the vodka, sliced limes and ice cubes.

Yields about twenty 4 oz (125 mL) servings.

# Cranberry Juice

When cranberries are on special in the fall, buy a lot of them, make this juice and have a winter's supply of breakfast drinks. It's also good diluted with ginger ale or used as the base for a fruit punch.

8 cups (2 L) cranberries
8 cups (2 L) water
1½ cups (375 mL) granulated
    sugar or ¾ cup (175 mL)
    liquid clover honey

Pour the berries and water into a large saucepan. Cover and bring to the boil over high heat. Reduce heat and simmer until the berries are tender, about 8 minutes. Mash and continue cooking another 2 minutes.

Wet a jelly bag, wring it out and fill with the cranberry mixture. Let the juice drip out, then press and twist the jelly bag to extract as much juice as possible.

Pour the juice into a clean saucepan. Add the sweetening; taste and add more if desired. Bring to the boil over high heat. Boil 1 minute.

Pour into hot clean canning jars, leaving a ¼" (6 mm) headspace. Process in a canner for 15 minutes (see page 89). Makes about 10 to 12 cups (2.5 to 3 L) juice.

To serve, combine 2 parts juice and 1 part cold water or soda water. Add a few ice cubes and a slice of orange.

Yields fifteen to eighteen 8 oz (250 mL) servings.

# Raspberry Acid

Tartaric acid is easily bought in a drugstore.

6 cups (1.5 L) raspberries
1¾ cups (425 mL) cold water
4 tsp (20 mL) tartaric acid
4 cups (1 L) granulated sugar

Dump the berries into a medium-large glass, enamelled or plastic bowl. Crush. Combine the water and tartaric acid, pour over the berries, stir well and cover. Let stand 24 hours.

Strain, pressing to extract as much of the juice as possible. There should be about 3½ cups (875 mL) juice.

Pour the juice into a large saucepan (a large one is needed because the juice foams up unexpectedly high), stir in the sugar and bring to the boil over high heat. Boil vigorously 3 minutes; skim.

Fill hot sterilized canning jars to within ¼" (6 mm) of the top, cover and process 15 minutes in the canner (see page 89). Store in a cool dry place. Makes about 5 cups (1.25 L) syrup.

To serve, combine 1 part Raspberry Acid with 2 to 3 parts cold water or soda water and a few ice cubes in a tall glass. Stir. Add a sprig of mint and a fresh raspberry, if available.

Yields fifteen to twenty 8 oz (250 mL) servings.

# Raspberry Brandy

4 cups (1 L) raspberries
3 cups (750 mL) brandy
1 cup (250 mL) granulated sugar

Mash or purée the raspberries. Combine with the brandy and pour into a plastic or glass container with an airtight lid. Store in the refrigerator 1 week, stirring the mixture once a day.

Wet a jelly bag, wring it out and fill it with the raspberry mixture. Press out all the juice. Mix in the sugar and stir until it dissolves. Pour into clean bottles and cap.

Yields 5 cups (1.25 L).

# Strawberry Brandy

Proceed as for Raspberry Brandy, but use 8 cups (2 L) strawberries.

# Rhubarb Nectar

Positively one of the best liked old-time summer drinks coast to coast —
maybe because rhubarb is so easy to grow. Combined with spices and
orange, it certainly makes a very refreshing drink. Try to use the pinkest
rhubarb.

| | |
|---|---|
| 12 cups (3 L) chopped rhubarb, in 1" (2.5 cm) pieces | 4" (10 cm) piece cinnamon stick (approximate) |
| 4 cups (1 L) water | 3 cups (750 mL) granulated sugar (approximate) |
| 1 lemon | |
| 1 orange | |

Place the rhubarb and water in a large preserving kettle. Pare the zest off
the lemon and orange; crush the cinnamon lightly and add it with the
zests to the kettle.

Bring to the boil over high heat, then reduce the heat, stir, cover and
simmer 10 minutes. The rhubarb should be well broken up. Wet a jelly
bag and wring it out. Strain the rhubarb mixture through the bag.
Squeeze out as much juice as possible. There should be 6 cups (1.5 L).
Pour into a large saucepan and add ½ cup (125 mL) sugar for each cup
(250 mL) juice. Squeeze the lemon and orange, and strain their juice
into the saucepan. Stir well. Bring to the boil and boil 3 minutes. For use
within 2 weeks, pour into hot sterile jars, seal, cool and store in the
refrigerator. For longer, safer storage, pour the boiling syrup into hot
sterilized canning jars, leaving ¼" (6 mm) headspace, adjust lids and
process 15 minutes in a canner (see page 89). Makes 8 cups (2 L) nectar.

To serve, combine with equal amounts of cold soda water. Add ice, a
slice of orange and a sprig of mint.

Yields sixteen 8 oz (250 mL) servings.

# Raspberry Juice

16 cups (4 L) raspberries
8 cups (2 L) water
2 cups (500 mL) granulated sugar

Pour the raspberries into a preserving kettle in several batches, crushing each layer. Add the water and cover. Bring to the boil over high heat. Reduce the heat and simmer 15 minutes. Crush periodically to extract all the juice.

Wet a jelly bag and wring it out. Pour the raspberry pulp and juice into the bag and let drip out 3 to 4 hours. If you squeeze to get any remaining juice, there will be some sediment in the syrup.

Combine the juice and sugar in a large saucepan. Bring to the boil over high heat. Pour into hot canning jars, leaving a ¼" (6 mm) headspace; seal and process in the canner for 15 minutes (see page 89). Makes 10 cups (2.5 L) syrup.

To serve, mix 2 parts juice with 1 part cold water or soda water and a few ice cubes. Decorate each glass with a sprig of mint and/or a fresh berry. Yields fifteen 8 oz (250 mL) servings.

# Strawberry Soda

Sodas have slipped out of fashion — temporarily, I hope. No soda is as pretty as a strawberry soda, especially with a whole unhulled berry on top. Strawberry syrup is available in supermarkets.

2 Tbs (30 mL) hulled crushed
  strawberries
1 Tbs (15 mL) granulated sugar
2 Tbs (25 mL) strawberry syrup

3 scoops good vanilla ice cream
  or Strawberry Ice Cream
  (page 82)
⅔ cup (150 mL) chilled soda
  water
1 unhulled strawberry

Combine the berries, sugar and syrup. Stir to dissolve the sugar. Pour about a third of this into a soda glass or any tall narrow 1½ cup (375 mL) glass, add a scoop of the ice cream, another third of the strawberry mixture, another scoop of the ice cream, the rest of the strawberry mixture, then the last scoop of ice cream. Gently pour the soda water into the glass, top with the whole berry and serve immediately.

Yields 1 big soda.

# Strawberry Champagne Punch

Hans Wien, who owns a small fruit farm in Prince Edward County, Ontario, generously contributed this family punch recipe. It's perfect for an early summer wedding.

½ cup (125 mL) water
½ cup (125 mL) orange juice
½ cup (125 mL) granulated sugar
2 cups (500 mL) hulled sliced
  strawberries
1 orange, thinly sliced

1 bottle (750 mL) white wine
1 tray ice cubes
1 cup (250 mL) small unhulled
  strawberries
1 bottle (750 mL) chilled
  champagne

Combine the water, orange juice, sugar, sliced strawberries and orange in a large bowl. Stir and mash lightly. Pour in the white wine. Cover and leave at room temperature for 4 hours. Stir and mash periodically to extract all the flavour from the fruit. Strain and chill thoroughly. This may all be done a day in advance and stored in the refrigerator.

To serve, pour the strawberry-flavoured wine into a punch bowl, add the ice cubes, whole strawberries and finally the champagne. Serve while still fizzing. Multiply the recipe according to length of drinking time and number of guests. Yields 2 glasses each for 6 to 8 people.

# Berry Buttermilk

Something good for the kids. Add an egg and it's breakfast in a hurry. The buttermilk gives this drink quite a refreshing tang.

½ cup (125 mL) raspberries,
  blueberries, or hulled
  strawberries
½ tsp (3 mL) grated lemon or
  orange rind

1 tsp (5 mL) lemon or orange
  juice
2 Tbs (25 mL) liquid clover honey
2 cups (500 mL) buttermilk
2 mint sprigs

Combine the berries, rind, juice and honey in a food processor or blender. Whirl until blended. Pour in the buttermilk and whirl again, just until mixed.

An alternate method that does not require a machine and that eliminates the seeds is simply to press the fruit through a food mill or sieve, then beat the purée into the rind, juice, honey and buttermilk.

Pour into 2 large glasses. Garnish with mint.

Yields 2 servings.

# Raspberry Milkshake

Make shakes in the winter with frozen berries; if they have been sweetened, just leave out the honey in the recipe.

½ cup (125 mL) raspberries
1 tsp (5 mL) liquid clover honey
2 large scoops good vanilla ice
  cream
¾ cup (175 mL) homogenized
  milk

Purée the berries and honey in a blender or a food processor. Add the ice cream and milk and whirl until the shake is thick and smooth. Pour immediately into a tall chilled glass and serve.

Yields 1 large shake.

# Strawberry Milkshake

Substitute hulled strawberries for the raspberries in Raspberry Milkshake.

# Purple Cow

Substitute ⅔ cup (150 mL) blueberries for the raspberries in Raspberry Milkshake.

# SUMMER SOUPS AND SAVOURIES

## Red Currant and Raspberry Soup

This fruit soup, like the others that follow, can either begin or end the meal.

| | |
|---|---|
| 4 cups (1 L) stemmed red currants | ⅓ cup (75 mL) granulated sugar |
| 2 cups (500 mL) raspberries | ¾ cup (175 mL) sour cream or |
| 1 cup (250 mL) water | whipped cream |

Combine the fruit and water in a saucepan. Bring to the boil, reduce the heat and simmer until the fruit is very tender, about 5 to 8 minutes.

Extract all the juice and pulp by pressing through a fine sieve or a food mill fitted with the fine disk. While the soup is still hot, add the sugar and taste; add more sugar if desired, but the soup should be tart. Cool, cover and chill.

To serve, pour into individual bowls and swirl in a big dollop of the cream.

Yields 4 small servings.

## Red Currant Soup

Proceed as for Red Currant and Raspberry Soup, substituting 2 cups (500 mL) more stemmed red currants for the raspberries. Serve hot or cold.

# Cranberry and Apple Soup

6 cups (1.5 L) Cranberry Juice (page 111)
1 cup (250 mL) peeled cored diced apples, Northern Spy recommended
1 tsp (5 mL) grated lemon rind
2 Tbs (25 mL) cornstarch
¼ cup (50 mL) granulated sugar
1 cup (250 mL) sour cream or whipped cream

Pour the juice into a saucepan; add the apples and lemon rind. Bring to the boil. Reduce the heat and simmer 5 minutes, or until the apple cubes are tender but not broken up.

Blend the cornstarch into the sugar, stir into the soup and cook, stirring gently, until the mixture thickens and clears. Taste; add more sugar if desired. Cool, cover and chill.

To serve, pour into individual bowls and swirl in a big dollop of cream.

Yields 6 servings.

# Summer Rhubarb Soup

3 cups (750 mL) chopped rhubarb, in ½″ (12 mm) pieces
½ cup (125 mL) raisins
¼ tsp (1 mL) ground allspice
⅛ tsp (0.5 mL) freshly grated nutmeg
3 cups (750 mL) water
1 cup (250 mL) red wine
4 tsp (20 mL) cornstarch
¾ cup (175 mL) granulated sugar
thin outer zest of ½ orange
½ cup (125 mL) sour cream

Combine the rhubarb, raisins, spices, 2 cups (500 mL) of the water and the wine in a large saucepan. Cover and bring to the boil over high heat, then reduce the heat to low and simmer very gently until the rhubarb is tender, about 5 minutes. Remove from the heat.

Blend the cornstarch into the sugar, then stir into the rhubarb and cook uncovered, over medium heat, until the soup thickens and clarifies. Stir frequently. Cool.

Pour the soup into individual bowls, cover and chill.

Cut the orange zest into fine slivers. Combine with the remaining 1 cup (250 mL) water in a small saucepan and bring to the boil. Reduce the heat and simmer 3 minutes. Drain, discard the water and pat the zest dry between towelling. Reserve.

To serve, spoon a dollop of sour cream onto each serving of soup and sprinkle the cream with the slivered orange zest.

Yields 6 to 8 servings.

# Cranberry Vegetable Pot Roast

From the provincial archives in Victoria, British Columbia, an idea that adds colour and piquancy to a family meal. Serve this roast, with its luscious rich brown sauce, with a big bowl of whipped parsley potatoes and crisp green beans, brussels sprouts or broccoli.

3 ½ to 4 ½ lb (1.75 to 2 kg) boned pot roast
2 Tbs (25 mL) oil
2 cups (500 mL) coarsely chopped onions
1 clove garlic, chopped
¾ cup (175 mL) chopped carrots
½ cup (125 mL) chopped celery
1 cup (250 mL) cranberries
1 Tbs (15 mL) liquid clover honey
1 tsp (5 mL) salt
½ tsp (3 mL) freshly ground pepper
3 parsley stalks

1 bay leaf
½ tsp (3 mL) crushed dried summer savory
1 tsp (5 mL) Dijon mustard
⅛ tsp (0.5 mL) ground allspice
2" (5 cm) strip of orange peel
½ cup (125 mL) red wine
½ cup (125 mL) beef stock

GRAVY:
1 Tbs (15 mL) flour
1 Tbs (15 mL) soft butter

Dry the roast all over. Pour the oil into a deep heavy-bottomed saucepan just large enough to accommodate the meat. Heat the oil; when a drop of water sizzles and bounces in it, add the meat and brown well on all sides. Use wooden spoons to turn the meat.

Remove the meat, add the chopped vegetables and cook over medium heat 4 to 5 minutes. Nestle the meat among the vegetables and add all the remaining ingredients except those for the gravy. Heat to boiling; cover, but leave the lid slightly ajar, and immediately reduce the heat so that the roast simmers gently, about 2 to 2½ hours, or until tender. Turn the roast with the wooden spoons every 30 minutes.

To serve, remove the roast to a warm platter; cover and set in a warm place. Remove the bay leaf and orange peel. Blend the sauce, or pass through a food mill or sieve, and return to the saucepan. Mash the flour and soft butter together and whisk into the gravy. Return to the heat and cook 3 to 4 minutes to thicken evenly. Taste and add more seasoning if desired.

Pour about a cup (250 mL) of the sauce over the roast and pass the rest separately to serve over vegetables.

Yields 6 servings.

# Cranberry Glazed Loin of Pork

This is a show-off roast, excellent for a dinner party. For looks, choose a centre cut or rib end roast, but to get the succulent tenderloin, choose the loin end. Make sure to have the backbone sawed at ¾" (2 cm) intervals to make carving easy.

For a boned and rolled double loin roast, proceed as below with the following exceptions: stick the strips of orange peel into the centre, all along the roast, between the two loins. Roast on a rack and allow 5 to 10 minutes more per pound (0.5 kg).

Serve with a rich winter vegetable such as glazed carrots, squash or parsnips, or a purée of turnip and apple. Garnish the platter lavishly with watercress or parsley.

one 5 lb (2.25 kg) loin of pork, at room temperature
1 orange

¾ cup (175 mL) Classic Cranberry Sauce (page 76)
salt

GLAZE:
⅓ cup (75 mL) soft butter
2 tsp (10 mL) Dijon mustard
1 tsp (5 mL) flour
¼ tsp (2 mL) ground ginger
¼ tsp (2 mL) freshly ground pepper

GRAVY:
3 Tbs (45 mL) flour
2 Tbs (30 mL) soft butter
2 cups (500 mL) hot water or mild stock
salt and freshly ground pepper

Preheat oven to 325°F (160°C).

Cut the thin outer zest from the orange; poke strips of it into the meat in the spaces where the backbone has been sawed. Squeeze the juice out of the orange, strain and reserve for the gravy.

To prepare the glaze, combine the butter, mustard, flour, ginger and pepper. Spread this paste all over the meat. Set the roast, rib bone side down, in an open roasting pan and roast for 35 to 40 minutes per pound (0.5 kg).

After 1½ hours, remove the roast from the oven and spread the cranberry sauce evenly over the fat side. Continue roasting until done.

When the roast reaches an interior temperature of 180°F (82°C), remove from the oven and place on a warm platter. Sprinkle lightly with salt and cover loosely with foil; keep it warm. Let stand 10 minutes to allow the juices to retreat back into the fibres.

To prepare the gravy, drain the fat but not the brown drippings out of the roasting pan. Mash the flour and butter together and blend into the drippings, using a wooden spoon. Gradually blend in the orange juice, then the water. Whisk to obtain a smooth gravy. Make sure to scrape up all the tasty brown bits. Add salt and pepper to taste. Strain into a warmed gravy boat and serve over the carved meat.

Yields 6 generous servings.

# Cranberry Baked Pork Chops

If I hadn't already said in *Apples, Peaches & Pears* that apples were created to go with pork, I could now say that cranberries definitely were.

| | |
|---|---|
| 6 medium pork chops, about ¾″ (2 cm) thick | ¼ cup (50 mL) liquid clover honey |
| ½ tsp (3 mL) salt | 2 cups (500 mL) cranberries |
| ¼ tsp (2 mL) freshly ground pepper | ¼ tsp (1 mL) ground cloves |
| 1 cup (250 mL) chopped onions | ½ tsp (3 mL) freshly grated nutmeg |
| ½ cup (125 mL) dry white or red wine, or cider | 1 Tbs (15 mL) soft butter |
| | 1 Tbs (15 mL) flour |

Preheat oven to 325°F (160°C).

Trim the excess fat off the chops. Slash in two or three places through the fat along the round side, to prevent curling.

Transfer the trimmed fat to a large frying pan and heat at a medium setting until about 3 Tbs (45 mL) of the fat has melted. Discard the remaining crisped fat. Increase the heat to high and brown the chops on both sides. Place them in a single layer in a shallow heatproof dish. Season with salt and pepper. Reserve.

Add the onions to the frying pan, sauté over medium heat until translucent but not browned, and spread over the chops. Drain off any remaining fat. Pour the wine and honey into the frying pan and heat, scraping up all the brown bits.

Distribute the cranberries over the onions, then pour the pan liquid evenly over all. Sprinkle on the spices.

Cover tightly and bake for 40 to 45 minutes, or until the meat is tender.

Remove the chops, with their onion and berry topping, to a heated platter. Cover and keep warm.

If the baking dish cannot be used on top of the stove, pour all the pan juices from the baking dish into a saucepan. Scrape up any brown bits. Blend together the butter and flour. Heat the pan juices at a medium setting and whisk in a little of the butter-flour paste at a time, until the sauce thickens enough to coat a spoon. Keep the rest of the paste refrigerated to thicken other gravies and sauces. Taste and adjust the seasoning if necessary. Cook 2 to 3 minutes more and pour over the chops.

Yields 6 servings.

# Roast Chicken with Gooseberry Sauce

From the Ukrainian-Canadian tradition, a classic roast chicken with a sauce that combines the tartness of the gooseberries with the savour of chicken and a touch of smooth creaminess. Serve with buttered noodles and a bowl of garden peas, the sugar-pod variety if possible.

one 5 lb (2.25 kg) roasting
   chicken, at room temperature
¾ cup (175 mL) roughly chopped
   onions
1 cup (250 mL) roughly chopped
   celery leaves and stalks
2 bay leaves
4 sage leaves or 1 tsp (5 mL)
   crushed dried sage
1 Tbs (15 mL) slivered lemon
   zest

1 tsp (5 mL) salt
¼ tsp (2 mL) freshly ground pepper
3 Tbs (45 mL) melted butter

SAUCE:
2 Tbs (30 mL) butter
2 cups (500 mL) gooseberries
3 Tbs (45 mL) liquid clover honey
¼ tsp (2 mL) salt
⅓ cup (75 mL) heavy cream

Preheat oven to 425°F (220°C).

Wipe the chicken inside and out with a clean damp cloth. Toss together the onions, celery, herbs, zest, ½ tsp (3 mL) of the salt and pepper. Stuff lightly into the body and neck cavities. (This is not an "eating" stuffing, but simply a "flavouring" stuffing.) Truss the chicken and set on a rack in an open roasting pan. Brush all over with the melted butter, reserving any that remains for preliminary basting.

Roast for 15 minutes, then reduce heat to 350°F (180°C) and roast about 1½ hours more. Baste periodically, first with the butter and then with the pan juices. About 15 minutes before the end of the roasting time sprinkle on the remaining salt.

The chicken is done when the skin on the breast turns crisp and golden and puffs up. The drumstick will also jiggle loosely. A further test is to stick a skewer into the thickest part of the thigh; if the juices run clear the chicken is done. The interior temperature of the thickest part of the thigh should register 190°F (88°C). Transfer to a heated platter and let stand 10 minutes, to allow the juices to be absorbed back into the flesh.

To make the sauce in the meantime, melt the butter. Add the gooseberries and sauté 5 to 8 minutes, or until tender. Add the honey and salt. Purée and return to a clean saucepan.

When the chicken is finished, skim all the fat off the roasting pan. There should be about ½ cup (125 mL) of brown drippings. Add the drippings to the gooseberry sauce, heat through and stir in the cream. Taste. It might be necessary to add more honey, but the sauce should be tart to contrast with the crisp rich skin and juicy meat. Heat the sauce until it bubbles, pour it into a warmed sauceboat and serve over the carved chicken.

Yields 6 very generous servings.

# Thrimble

A Newfoundland dish of pork chops stuffed with a savoury mixture of apples, cranberry sauce and spices, sautéed and braised in white wine.

6 pork chops, ¾" (2 cm) thick, from the centre or the rib end

STUFFING:
¼ cup (50 mL) butter
¼ cup (50 mL) finely chopped onion
1½ cups (375 mL) peeled cored chopped apples
½ tsp (3 mL) salt
¼ tsp (2 mL) freshly ground pepper
⅛ tsp (0.5 mL) cinnamon
⅛ tsp (0.5 mL) ground cloves

⅔ cup (150 mL) Classic Cranberry Sauce (page 76)
1⅓ cups (325 mL) cubes of stale but still soft homemade-style bread

SAUCE:
1 cup (250 mL) white wine or chicken stock
1 tsp (5 mL) cider vinegar
salt and freshly ground pepper

Trim the fat evenly from the pork chops, leaving a ¼" (6 mm) band around the curved side. Keep the trimmings. With a very sharp pointed knife, slit the chops horizontally, from end to end and right to the bone, to form a generous pocket. Reserve.

Put the pork fat trimmings into a large frying pan over medium heat and render out ¼ cup (50 mL) liquid fat. Discard the crisp scraps and reserve the rendered fat in the frying pan.

Melt the butter in a medium frying pan over medium heat. Add the onions, apples, salt and spices; sauté about 5 to 8 minutes, or until the onions and apples are tender. Turn into a large bowl; add the cranberry sauce and bread cubes. Toss together and cool enough to handle. Taste and adjust seasoning if desired. Spoon a sixth of the stuffing into the pocket of each chop. Fasten the sides together with toothpicks. The chops will look very chubby.

Heat the reserved fat over a medium-high setting and brown the chops quickly on both sides. Skim off and discard the fat, but not the brown drippings. Add the wine and vinegar, cover and simmer 30 minutes. Turn the chops after 15 minutes and set the lid of the pan slightly ajar to let the sauce reduce.

Place the chops on a warmed platter, remove the toothpicks, cover and keep warm. Boil the pan juices over high heat until reduced and thickened. Taste; add salt and pepper if desired. Spoon over the chops. Serve immediately. Yields 6 servings.

# INDEX

## Miscellaneous